PRAISE FOR JUSTIN ROSS LEE

"Even when he's at his ugliest, he's beautifully dressed."
—*New York Times*

"Car-crash ability to piss people off." —*New York Post*

"His hacks are equal parts ingenious and outrageous."
—*Nightline*, ABC News

"Savvy travel hacker." —Stephen Colbert

"Travels all around the world, eating good food, staying fancy."
—Wendy Williams

"Three things he never pays for: parking, publicity and pussy."
—*New York Observer*

Don't
You Know
Who I Think
I Am?

Don't You Know Who I Think I Am?

Confessions of a First-Class Asshole

JUSTIN ROSS LEE

INKSHARES

Published by Inkshares, Inc., San Francisco, California
www.inkshares.com

Cover design by David Drummond
© gualtiero boffi/Shutterstock, © Ivan Cholakov/Shutterstock,
© Viorel Sima/Shutterstock, © grandboat/Shutterstock

ISBN: 9781941758694
e-ISBN: 9781941758700
Library of Congress Control Number: 2015948590

First edition

Printed in the United States of America

A NOTE FROM THE GENERAL COUNSEL OF INKSHARES

On Inkshares, readers decide what gets published. This book, *Don't You Know Who I Think I Am? Confessions of a First-Class Asshole*, contains views that may be deemed misogynistic, obscene, and reprehensible. They do not reflect the views of Inkshares or its employees. They are solely the views of Mr. Lee, the self-styled "asshole" who wrote this book.

INTRODUCTION

INTRODUCTION? I NEED NO INTRODUCTION

I fucking hate when I'm asked, "So, what do you do?"

I find it painful to explain my vocation. I'm not really an asshole; I just play one on TV. To someone just meeting me, it can be a risky interaction. Explaining my anti-nine-to-five lifestyle tends to border on arrogance. Is this all an act? Hardly. I think of it as more of a performance.

Because I don't *do*; I *am*. This glorious, repellent, beautiful train wreck of a life is my own fabulous creation and gift to the world. You've seen me on Bravo's *The Millionaire Matchmaker*, gracing the pages of tabloids, trilled about in newspapers, featured on morning shows in Croatia, and causing American sensationalism in Sweden. Or, more likely, you haven't.

But that's just the dressing, just the richly decorated yarmulke on the beautiful Jew-fro of my existence.

So what is it I actually do?

I'm a pioneer in the field of social media celebrity. I keep my loyal band of online followers on a tight leash, feeding them intoxicating morsels of my incredible life, just enough to keep them wet and interested. I gauge what gets their dreidels hard, then give them more. Some of them love it, even want to marry me. Most of them hate it. And those are the ones I care about most—the haters. If they fucking hate my dumb, smug, pampered face but keep coming back to the table for seconds, if they love hating me, I've got 'em. Right there is my key demographic. "Treat them mean to keep them keen" is a motto I adhere to.

"So that's what you do? You stick shit on the Internet?"

No, again, I've lost you. That's just an ingredient in my special sauce. It propagates the fan base and moves things along. But that's not what I do. It's what everyone does. Everyone lives their life online, and they all need a leader. Someone to look at and admire. I play that role. But again, that's just a means to an end. Same as my fashion line.

"Ah, right, so you're in the fashion business?"

Sigh. I'm prone to tell people I'm a haberdasher. First, because that sounds incredibly pretentious. Second, because of conversations like this. Trying to explain my life to someone who holds a position of authority is like trying to get a free hand job from an arthritic—that is, pointless and painful. However, this approach comprises a decent shortcut when I'm trying to conclude a tedious exchange. And it's a slightly more diplomatic response than "Google me," although I *have* resorted to that one when I'm feeling frisky.

I run a successful company, Pretentious Pocket, that produces pocket squares rendered from the finest "Fuck You" silk. But again, it's a smoke screen. A way to make an impression on people, a device so they'll remember me. If you give someone a business card, they're probably going to toss it. Give them a beautiful, garish piece of silk in a presentation box and a handwritten note. It's something that pays dividends every time they see you. Trust me. It's a business, and it gets me things for free.

"Why do you need things for free when you're so successful?"

Because successful people get things for free anyway. It's the fucked-up way of the world. Once you hit that level, people pay you to wear their clothes and eat their tea and crumpets. And, while some might see right through it, to others, I'm seen as a successful person. I've been sent $3,000 suits to wear and shirts to accompany them. I get free skin care and upgrades, and I'm comped meals and champagne. I'm sent luxury ice cubes. Ice cubes! Ten dollars a pop. And I get paid *not* to go certain places. I've been invited and uninvited a half dozen times to the same event. That's when I feel successful, when I reach that level of polarization.

I'm on that level because I appear to be on that level. You may have seen me at exclusive events, on the red carpet, spilling expensive drinks on Cuba Gooding Jr. I've made it my mission to mock celebrity in order to become a celebrity. It's not about legitimacy; it's the appearance of legitimacy. All the bullshit I did to get pictures taken with celebrities? People now pull that shit on me. Because, just like me, they don't really care about meeting someone. What they *really* care about is possessing the evidence of having met someone, especially a celebrated someone. That evidence is worth a thousand drunken anecdotes. That's why I'd rather leave my testicles at home than my camera.

"So you're a photographer?"

No, dumbass, I make sure that my exploits are exploited, which means they have to be documented. If I'm in an Emirates

A380 first-class cabin, then I want the world to know about it. I want them titillated. I want them salivating. I want them to see how much Dom I downed and caviar I spooned.

"So you like to fly?"

I, Justin Ross Lee, am the instigator and leading proponent of JewJetting. Allow me to explain. For generations, people have flown just to get from one place to another. With Jew-Jetting, the flight experience is the thing—tracking down and embarking on an airplane ride of such unimaginable opulence that the dummies in coach would gag with envy on their dry, chalky pretzels.

JewJetting is the sport of flying for the sake of it; the destination is of little importance. Do you think I want to go to Kiev? Fuck no! No one wants to go to Kiev unless they're selling Kevlar. But if some new carrier has launched a first-class cabin with ermine throw pillows, a foot massager, and a free foie gras dispenser, then I'd be the first one checking in. I love the mystery, energy, and satisfaction of luxury air travel. Besides, when I do it, it seems to piss off a lot of the people I want to piss off.

And now I know you're going to ask the other fucking question I hate: "But how can you afford to do all this?"

Sigh. There are a few common misconceptions about me. There always are when you're dealing with a person of interest. Was I born with a silver spoon in my mouth? Yes, definitely. Did I experience privilege? Absolutely. Did that experience give me a leg up in life? Sure, why not? However, not quite in the way you might think. (And incidentally, those privileged people fucking hate me, too.)

The well-heeled I had the unfortunate experience of growing up amongst do have money, but that's usually all they do with it. They have it. They don't enjoy it. In fact, it terrifies them. They simply abide by a predetermined prescription for acquiring and maintaining excess. They fear that if they stray from the tediously conventional path, they'll be punished, or singled out. People such as these forced me to create the legend I am today—whereby I'm proud to say that I've circumvented my own circumcision in order to escape the bullshit. My lifestyle is the ultimate revenge. Hi, Mom!

My current endeavors are not trust-funded. My family is as mortified as anyone by what I do. They're not going to give me a dime. Despite appearances, I don't give a shit about money. I think of money as I do of everything else around me: as a means to an end. If I hit Powerball tomorrow, would I carry on doing what I do? Totally. Because what I'm doing is being JRL. No amount of bullion can interfere with that. Attention is the only currency I trade in, good or bad. Preferably bad. Negative attention brings positive results.

"So you want people to hate you?" you might inquire.

Given my lifestyle, it can't be helped. It does tend to piss people off. If you actually *work* for a living and pay for stuff, you don't want to hear about a jerk like me who just metaphorically whips out his dick online and doesn't have to pay for anything. So what should I do? Stop flying, drinking, and dating beautiful women? Stop appearing at exclusive nightclubs and restaurants while people pay me for the privilege? Just to keep some office drones happy? Joke's on Jew!

"Oh? You're Jewish?"

Wow, you *are* sharp. I'm "super Jewish" according to the *New York Post*. It's another buzzy shortcut to annoying people. They see me as this overcompensated, arrogant, pretentious, spoiled little putz. Exactly what I aspire to be, and I can't think of anything more beautiful.

You might deem my ridiculously short workweek and general flaneurism rampant underachieving. Correction: it's rampant *overunderachieving*. Minimum effort for maximum return. It's something I've excelled at for most of my life, and I'm happy to share my dirty little secrets with you.

"I don't think I understand."

Good. Then I've won.

CHAPTER 1

MY JEWLOSOPHY

April 11, 2008

Pastis was a nauseatingly popular eating establishment located in Manhattan's overly legendary meatpacking district. For those of you unfortunate enough to live in one of the flyover states, the meatpacking district is where (1) by day, burly men once packed meat into trucks for delivery, and (2) by night, other men packed meat into each other. In the 1990s, the bottom fell out of both markets and the area slowly gentrified into the overpriced nightmare it is today.

At the time of my Pastis incident, I was lost. Hard to believe, I know, looking at the phenomenon I have now become. But true. Yes, I was a dick, an exemplary dick. I'd recently been fired from the only job I'd ever had. I lasted four days. (In grad school, they are very effective at teaching you how to get a job, but not necessarily how to keep one.) It seems the rest of the world understands that you don't write defamatory things about your superiors and colleagues for all to see on Facebook. I must have slept through that class. I shot my mouth off online and got canned.

I swiftly realized I was professionally unhireable. I'd had an inkling before that first dismissal, an assumption that I wasn't exactly suited for the everyday world of work. However, I had, until then, lacked the opportunity to test my assumption.

Sure enough, not long after I was given a keycard and directions to the photocopier, I screwed up and was out on my ass.

In my short tenure at my job, I learned that to succeed in the workplace, you have to conform. In fact, that's pretty much all you have to do. (It also helps to refrain from Facebook critiques of your colleagues.) In my visits to the offices of major film studios, national newspapers, and global media outlets, I've seen mostly people who are carbon masses with no discernible talent except the ability to be affable and sit behind a desk without catching fire. Unsurprisingly, some of these people have the word "executive" as part of their title.

I was not one of them. I was never going to be one of them.

I am a grade A nonconformist. Since my diaper-shitting days, I've done all I can to provoke, annoy, and infuriate. While these are not valued skills in the workplace, they are essential components of my nature. The thought of me getting a job and sitting in some dinky office space for a decade, signing a card for Gloria's birthday, or heading to Applebee's for an end-of-the-week celebration lunch on Friday makes me want to open a vein. I'd purposefully developed special skills in my young life to avoid precisely that. During boarding school and college, I'd honed those skills. I'd designed systems and practices to subvert every establishment that tried to contain me. It was what

I was good at. My one problem was how to monetize what I was good at.

So there I stood in front of Pastis on a beautiful spring day, regretfully looking at the outside seating area, where one couldn't get a reservation no matter how many dicks one sucked. It was one of the most exclusive restaurants in Manhattan at the time, and I felt like the lowliest schmuck on the Lower East Side. In my dire state of unemployment, that exalted level of dining was a mere fantasy for the likes of me. The whiff of failure permeated the air around me like cheap cologne on a New York cab driver with a three-syllable name.

I approached the maître d's podium with my two companions, both members of the elite Jew Live Crew, and resigned myself to the fate of a dingy table next to the crapper. If we were lucky. The maître d' was already regarding me like the trash I felt like. His mouth was already forming the word "no" before I'd even opened my yapper. I very often have that effect on people. Before we even engage, they've established an opinion about me, usually a negative one. (It can be tiresome but, read on, also extremely beneficial.)

Suddenly something stirred inside me. I became hyper-aware of my surroundings, instantly cognizant of certain props within my grasp that could be employed for the creation of mayhem. On the podium was a water glass. I knew right away what to do. Before identifying myself, I reached for a matchbook cover and, with a sweep of my Zegna cuff, knocked the glass to the ground, where it shattered.

Pandemonium ensued, as it tends to in this type of establishment when something goes awry and the perfectly ordered infrastructure derails. Servers appeared, brooms were brandished, and importantly, backs were turned away from the podium to attend to the disaster.

I began to apologize profusely in the manner of a drunken guest who has accidentally shit on the seder plate. And while the staff was occupied, I seized my opportunity, leaned over the podium, and snuck a look at the reservation list. I instinctively knew two things were important: the time and party size. Anything else was irrelevant. Which is why, when order was finally restored, I found myself saying, "Yes, reservation for three. Paglieri's the name."

Now, I don't look like a Paglieri. Maybe Paglieristein or Pagliberg would be more convincing. But the management just wanted this fucking glass smasher out of their hair as quickly as possible. A flustered hostess grabbed a couple of menus and led us away.

We were seated at an outside table. Scratch that; we were seated at the *best* outside table. The best fucking table at the most desirable location in New York.

We ordered drinks in an atmosphere of mild hysteria. My companions were completely confused, but I just told them to go with it and be sure to call me Benito within earshot of the maître d'.

Our order arrived, and we seemed to have pulled it off. It was all going *swimmingly*—when out of the corner of my eye I caught the unmistakably erect posture of a restaurant general manager approaching at speed. If I could describe his gait, it would be something like a swift, panicked glide. He stood beside me at the table and hovered there as if I had just scratched his Fiat.

"Mr. Paglieri?"

"Yes?" I replied, possibly with the slightest hint of a Tuscan accent.

"It seems there is a problem . . ."

"No problems at all. The service has been excellent. Myself and my companions are highly satisfied. Thanks for stopping by."

I turned back to my friends and continued chatting, gesticulating in a characteristically Mediterranean way.

The general manager held his post. "No, sir, I really must speak to you," he said firmly.

"Can I get some more ice when you get a chance?" I said nonchalantly.

The bullshit just naturally flowed from me. My fellow diners looked on with openmouthed expressions that I imagine most people make when watching *2 Girls 1 Cup*.

"Sir, I was wondering if I could possibly see some identification?"

"Well, I'm flattered, obviously. Thank you for the compliment, but this is a *virgin* iced tea. We were considering some wine with our meal. Is there anything you'd recommend?"

I think I could see the real Mr. Paglieri loitering by the podium and growing increasingly frantic. He looked like a more volatile Tony Soprano, and I wondered if I should have stolen a less ethnic name.

"Sir, you are obviously not the man you have claimed to be. I will have to insist you leave immediately."

"We are very comfortable here, thank you. Is Andre working today?"

My disinterested, calm tones were really unnerving him. He wasn't exactly angry, but rather more exasperated. And bemused, completely thrown off by a would-be customer trying such a poorly thought-out prank and counting on the manager's apparent stupidity. It was slowly dawning on him that this wasn't some bizarre misunderstanding, but instead a deliberate, premeditated con job.

"Why? Why did you do this?" His voice was strained, like a parent who has just discovered his kid Crayola-ing the living room wall.

"Well, obviously, because I didn't have a reservation and I wanted to sit here. Is that so unreasonable?"

My companions were loving this. The general manager continued to linger and began to display the seven stages of customer service grief: pleading, then shouting, then cajoling, then joking, then more shouting, then crying, then threatening to call the cops.

We didn't care. We refused to budge. There were drinks before us, the pleasure of an exceptional meal awaited us, and we had less to lose than he did. At this point, I became really interested in how far I could stretch this. We weren't doing anything illegal. Slightly rude, possibly—OK, incredibly rude— but, *oy* fucking *vey*, I thought. It's not like we were planning to dine and dash. We were going to pay live American currency, and surely the real Mr. Paglieri would be happy to be seated on the mezzanine.

Unfortunately, we'd burrowed too deep under the skin of this man, our general manager. When he retreated, I could see him anxiously making a phone call. And right about then, I decided I didn't want to be dragged out of there like a whore from church just for the sake of a few yuks. We had to end our adventure. Immediately.

After hurling my napkin to the table with a flourish, I stormed out, spouting a raft of nasty epithets in my wake as we exited. I imagine Marie Antoinette could not have done it with more aplomb as she left her cell en route to the guillotine.

"What you did today was unconscionable," the manager had spat at us as we walked out with our heads held high.

We all received lifetime bans from the restaurant, of course. Though, because they knew me as Mr. Paglieri and nothing else, I don't know how they planned to enforce the ban.

The Pastis incident set off a fascinating revelation for me.

Criminals tend to be impulsive and incapable of empathy. Why? For the rush, that sensation you feel when you embark on something illicit and you completely get away with it. I felt the same rush on that day at Pastis. Except my crime was completely legal. Sure, they'd threatened to call the cops, but even then, what could they do? Book us on a charge of impersonating a reservation? Hardly a justifiable collar for the NYPD. They'd just sigh and roll their eyes and shoot dirty looks at the general manager as they led us to the sidewalk and set us free.

I was glad I got caught. Sure, if we'd gotten away with it, we'd have had a delightful meal and a chuckle. But the discovery of our complicity blew this crisis into a drama. In addition to the thrill I felt, I had a story to go along with it. This is what I'd been searching for and unable to find. A legal con, just like this one. A social grift that has no repercussions. A kick against the societal conventions that I'd never adhered to anyway, a way of breaking laws that aren't on the books.

This time I'd fucked up and gotten busted. But, with a bit of planning, I knew I could pull off that kind of shit using my curious brand of bravado. With this kind of caper, the only thing I might suffer, if exposed, would be temporary embarrassment. Not really a problem. I don't get embarrassed. I don't feel shame. I've somehow managed to expel those feelings from my emotional repertoire.

My incipient love for social crime began to blossom. Getting noticed, being singled out, garnering attention. I *loved* it. It was something I'd dabbled with at school, initially for survival, and then, well, just for the hell of it. It was a kind of performance art—except that phrase makes me want to wrench my pelvis through my throat.

It was just me. But *me* times a million, my character turned into a character, a caricature of myself being me. A billboard that's not just outside your apartment window but sitting in your living room all the time, every day, advertising yours truly. A celebrity with none of the legwork.

I consider myself a sit-down comedian. That's a stand-up comedian, but with less substance abuse. I wanted attention and all the trappings that went along with it. But I didn't want to be doing an open-mike slot at the Laugh Factory at four thirty in the morning. Or be out in Hollywood standing in line, headshot in hand, trying to get a thirty-second walk-on on the new *90210*. I'd dipped my very talented toe into that world but soon lost curiosity. I'd discovered that the chances of me actually doing something interesting with that were dismally slim. I way prefer the instant gratification, the positive reinforcement, the *high* of making someone laugh.

I wanted to be a recognized face, but without paying all the dues—or any dues, actually. Hey, you think that sounds lazy and narcissistic? What about all those fucking wannabes on *American Idol*? Come on, if they really believed in themselves, they'd just go out and tour the toilets of middle America, delivering their cheesy take on soft rock. They could pay their dues the hard way, slowly clawing up that impossible ladder. But they choose to roll the dice and stick their faces on a TV talent show and hope they'll get lucky. Who can blame them? But, excuse me, artistic integrity? When you're warbling an Alanis Morissette tune to J-Lo? Probably as close as you can get to the complete opposite of artistic integrity. In my book, anyhow.

As for me, I wanted to perform. I just didn't have a format. Always a problem. I had a desire to entertain (I know, I'm so selfless; I just want to give), but the conventional route doesn't interest me. Like I said, I'm a nonconformist.

We think there's only one way you're allowed to be famous—the route movie stars, game-show hosts, and television personalities take. You can even be "famous for being famous." Fame is just another commodity. Like a house in the suburbs.

And the entertainment world bestows fame with a fickle finger. Once you've got it, you have to be always looking behind you, terrified that the younger, prettier version of you is coming up to snatch the food, and the pussy, out of your mouth. It's all designed to keep a prick like me in my place. I don't want to take orders and perform to someone else's satisfaction just to have a successful, if mediocre, career that might give me a shot at fame. I don't want to be documented on basic cable, then—because I show even the slightest hint of who I really am—be left to fade away and be forgotten. No thanks!

I want instant success and recognition with as little effort as possible, completely on my own terms, putting my completely unique, monetizable talents out there.

Sound impossible? Fuck you. Don't you know who I think I am?

I set about turning Justin Ross Lee into JRL. The cipher that would lead us to the promised land. "The ego that attacked New York," as the *New York Post* succinctly described me. "The most strategic swimmer in the social media cesspool," as the *New York Times* proclaimed, slightly more eloquently, and perhaps, accurately. A pure self-promoter who thrives on audience recognition and the media's incomprehensibility. They can't figure me out, which means they can't leave me alone. Just adds fuel to my subtle plans for world domination.

So, finally, I had my format. What happened at Pastis brought together all the various ingredients, and suddenly I saw the light. My name, my face, my obnoxiousness, my talent for getting bad press, my partying, my business interests, my love life, my JewJetting, and my social media presence. All I had to do was work each element against each other to keep the chemical reaction sparking along, to keep that weird alchemy of being here now and staying in the public eye, the public mind, for a long time. Piece of piss. I was born to do it.

There's more to it than that. There's no night school to learn this shit. You won't find it at the JCC. There were role models and sympathizers along the way, but I'm pretty much out here on my own. I had my natural instincts, and the rest I picked up and developed as I went along. Little systems and contingencies to cause the most mayhem and produce maximum exposure. Most of these I'll share with you; some I'll take to my grave. But it boils down to setting immediate goals and doing everything in your power to achieve them. Even if the prize is minuscule, it's not important. Hey, it's all about the journey toward the goal, right?

Just like in that restaurant. I wanted that table. I pitched a glass over. I got what I wanted. And then I figured out what I wanted to do with it.

Lesson 1: How to Be Hated

There are some people out there, sanctimonious types mainly, who consider goodness to be a virtue. There were a slew of them populating my hometown, growing up. They perpetuate the idea that if you can't say anything nice, you don't say anything at all.

I always tell my mother when I'm in the day's newspaper, and she always asks me the same question: "Is it good news?"

No, Mom. It's never good news. That's not the line I'm in. It's something of a harsh toke for her. Most people don't want to make waves; it seems unnatural. They want to drift through life without pissing people off, avoiding conflict at all turns. It's a great way to have zero drama and absolutely no intrigue in your life. If they were to appear in the press, it would be for some charitable deed or social contribution. The thought of hitting the headlines and being featured negatively would break their little hearts. From the second we splat out all over the delivery-room floor, we're looking for love and acceptance. Positive reinforcement. Not to be yelled at.

But once you clamber over that mental hurdle of acceptance and realize you don't have to be liked, it's incredibly liberating. The old adage that all press is good press holds up to a certain extent (unless you're caught trying to lure kids into your van or you're Mel Gibson). If you get in the paper for reaching your goal for the United Way, there will be a thumbnail-sized image of you lost on page 14, and that'll be it. If you're appearing due to some obnoxiously shitty thing you've said or done, it'll run and run. Especially if you keep adding fuel to the fire. The secret to Donald Trump's success . . .

Being nice and being liked are incredibly easy. You just basically have to stand there, smile, and not stab anyone. You have to be Mother Teresa, who I'm sure was a wonderful broad but would have never gotten a reservation at Smith & Wollensky. But to be hated and not immediately dismissed is a total tightrope walk. And it's a much, much harder approach to instigate and pull off. For every Howard Stern there are a dozen Charlie Sheens.

Personally, I think the margin has to be around 49 percent to 50 percent. Fifty percent liking me, 49 percent hating me, and a single percentage point who seems to do both. That's where I want to do all my business, in that 1 percent. The people driven crazy by my antics but who daren't look away. The gawkers. The ones who just can't put me down. I get under their skin and live there. Drives them crazy.

Of course, it's easy to hate me, and if you can't be bothered to find out the reason, joke's on Jew. There's more to me than being a simple hate figure—any douche bag could do that. I'm walking social satire over here, and if you don't get it, you can just keep strolling.

But it's so hard to balance. It's what I spend the majority of my time trying to decipher. Push things too far, pick on the wrong person, say the wrong thing, and people will just walk away. Tweak their buttons in just the right way, and they'll sit up and beg. If I'm spotted inside some splendid, luxurious nightclub sipping Cristal with some shiksa on my lap, the populace will just snort, roll their eyes, and bail. Show me getting kicked out of same nightclub, or refused entry because the doorman hates me and he pushes me over and steals my phone and I have a meltdown and call the cops, it creates a narrative. People might think I'm a complete ass, but they'll engage. They'll want to read to the end.

Generating this type of hate has been made so much easier thanks to social media. It's the perfect platform for picking bullshit fights. And people love it when you tackle the famous, even if it's manufactured. They don't care; they just want to see some blood on the canvas. It all has to do with pitch. You have to pick the right person to do battle with, and you need some evidence that it took place. A picture means everything. I can say I've picked a fight with whoever, but if there's a picture of me standing next to them, it adds legitimacy. You choose someone that people have heard of but don't care too much about. If they are beloved, they're instantly going to get all the sympathy. If they're despised, it's too easy a target.

If there's some perceived slight and I go after the latest degenerate bolstering *TMZ*'s ratings, it's win-win. If they engage and respond, fabulous. I can spin that out to a healthy amount of quotes and coverage. If they ignore me, even better. I can keep picking at that particular scab and have the focus be completely on myself. People make up their own minds about the celebs, their stance, and their particular peccadilloes. Everyone loves to take sides in a fight—it makes them feel engaged.

The people following this charade get to live vicariously through me. They'd love to be dickish to some hag from *The View*, but who gives a shit about their opinion? If I can get them nicely riled and foaming at the mouth on Twitter, followed up by a little piece in Page Six and a few scandalous quotes from yours truly, then effectively my job is done. You people love it. How do I know? You tell me. Not always directly, but that's the other beauty surrounding social media. There are tons of stats and graphs and analytics that tell me exactly when I've made your pussy wet.

I knew I'd made it in the hatred stakes when I started to be invited and uninvited to the same event multiple times. First, I'd be asked to attend; then someone else would call and tell me my presence would not be appreciated; then the first guy would call and apologize about the second guy; then I'd get a terse e-mail urging me to stay away; and then a car would arrive to pick me up. And either way I'd get paid. I was just turning up to drink champagne for fuck's sake.

It was then I knew I was doing something right.

CHAPTER 2

HITTING JEWBERTY

February 1999

It was winter in central New Hampshire, and it was as cold as fuck. At Brewster Academy, the fabulously expensive and privileged child prison in which I was interred, all the pupils were required to do sports. It was mandatory.

I don't do sports.

Sports make you *shvitz*. I'm not planning on sweating unless dinner, drinks, and light foreplay precedes it. I'm terrible at sports, so why would I bother? Let the lunkheads and pituitary cases enjoy their ball handling, and let me go and harass the baton twirlers or something. It was twenty below! And you want me to run out onto a frozen field while wearing shorts that leave nothing to the imagination?

I was just establishing my credentials as a fully fledged provocateur at Brewster, and the school was beginning to bitterly regret my existence. But being forced to take part in sports was still a problem. They were a big deal, elevated way beyond academic prowess. Laughable, really.

I knew I had to weasel out of it, but that meant dealing with the professionally asexual athletic director (Subaru Sue) and the dean of students (we'll call him Dean Doucheborn), with whom I shared a mutual loathing. He soon came to represent everything I hated about boarding school and was the perfect personification of the behavioral code I attempted to destroy from within. Needless to say, I was a pain in his prick.

Rather than take the route of perpetual illness or feigned injury, I knew I needed a more Machiavellian approach to get out of hockey or baseball or whatever the hell it was they did on that field out there. I arranged a summit between myself, Subaru Sue, and Dean Doucheborn, following all correct protocols and the proper procedure. I dressed as finely as school clothing rules allowed and collected the evidence I needed in a Tumi leather briefcase.

I displayed none of my usual bravado but entered the office and addressed them as if I were a salesman trying to get them to purchase my new line of urinal cakes.

"Thank you for seeing me," I intoned. "I would like to present you with an offer, which I feel will be beneficial to all of us."

They looked at me with the bored, impassive, unimpressed glare I'd come to earn from some of the faculty members of Brewster Academy.

"As you know, I am not particularly engrossed in the competitive sports offered here at Brewster, despite the excellence of the program."

I offered a distinguished nod to Subaru Sue, who nodded back, then looked annoyed when she realized she was joining in this ludicrous charade.

"But obviously, for the sake of school spirit and my own educational advancement, I desperately wish to participate in any way I can. And so, with that in mind, I'd hope you will carefully consider my proposal . . ."

I allowed a dramatic pause to be established. I think Doucheborn was about to throw a Jesus fish at me. I opened my briefcase and handed them both an embossed, professionally finished business card.

"I would like to offer my services to the school as the first student director of athletics."

They looked at the card sitting in their sweaty palms. It read "Justin R. Lee. Student Director of Athletics."

(Business cards are cheap, and they always impress.)

They both opened their mouths in reproach, so I continued quickly.

"This role will keep me highly occupied, and I promise to dedicate myself fully to the position. Obviously, with a demanding job like this, many of my other extracurricular activities will have to be curbed."

They looked at each other. They were considering whether to take the bribe. My inference was clear. If they let me take on this bullshit appointment, I would be less of a dick and total bane of their existence. I'd be too involved in my "directing" to indulge in my current routine of provocation and general dickishness.

"And what exactly would be involved as a director of student athletics?" Doucheborn asked.

"Student director of athletics," I corrected. "Ensuring that the health and safety requirements of my fellow students are upheld and that they are adequately hydrated at all times."

"Right . . . so . . . a water boy?"

"It might be considered that at lesser establishments, but I really would prefer the title of student director of athletics."

Both sighed. I could see Doucheborn attempting the calculations in his head. He wanted me out of his face as efficiently as possible. Then he took the bait.

"Fine. Whatever. Get out of here."

I thanked them both formally, closed my case, and exited.

And so I was appointed as Brewster Academy's first SDA (student director of athletics). Which was good, as I had five hundred business cards signaling this fact. Even for me, it was a pretty ballsy coup. As well as now being excused from all forms of physical activity, I knew that the job came with a very special perk. Doucheborn and Subaru Sue had made an error that would come to haunt them and cement my reputation as the biggest asshole that the school had ever encountered.

***

Boarding school proved to be the ideal environment for me. It provided the blueprint for everything I would go on to do in the future. With a perfectly defined structure of rules and conventions that I was able to subvert and manipulate, I quickly adapted, developing a particular range of skills. It's why I was excited to go there in the first place. Having run out of things to fight against at home, I needed more problems and regimes to wriggle out of. I needed to increase the gradient on the treadmill.

As far as I'm aware, I was a boringly satisfied kid. Rich, spoiled, Jewish. The classic combination. That all came screeching to a halt around my tenth birthday—incredibly, the exact moment of the change was documented. There's a picture of me sitting in the cockpit of a Boeing 727, wearing the pilot's hat and looking like the happiest fucking kid in the world. We were off on a family vacation, and, back before you'd be arrested for saying "box cutter" on a plane, I was invited into the cockpit, where this picture was taken.

It's an expression of relief I'm wearing in the image. Up to that point I had no idea what I wanted to do or to be. And in the community I grew up in, your role in life was designated pretty early on.

"You'll be a lawyer. You'll be a doctor. You'll be in business, just like Daddy."

All was prescribed and decided. And I felt that same pressure to conform, even though something inside me fought against it. So when I sat in the cockpit, all felt right. That's exactly what I wanted to do. I wanted to be a pilot. It made perfect sense. The glamour of it, the control. This was back when flying still had some mystery and cachet surrounding it, before planes became flying 7-Elevens. Plus I was spending every waking hour locked in my room, playing on a flight simulator. (This was prepuberty, obviously). It was cool to be a pilot; it impressed people. Except my parents.

When I told them of my intentions, they laughed in my face.

"A pilot? You can't be a pilot. We don't know any pilots. There aren't any Jewish pilots."

Who does that to a kid? Just humor me, for fuck's sake. But that was the problem. My loving parents don't have my sense of humor. It felt horrible, a massive disappointment. I felt ashamed, like someone had just wandered in and caught me jerking off. It was the same sensation.

I was never the same after that. My relationship with my parents degenerated. They'd changed me, they saw my vulnerability, and they could never empathize with me. I realized they were wrong, and that's pretty devastating for a kid. Even if I couldn't verbalize it, I knew that whatever I would be, it would be the exact opposite of what they wanted. If I couldn't be a pilot, then I'd be the best passenger the aeronautical industry had ever encountered. The rest of my life would be an extended revenge against their hopes and beliefs.

There were flashes of this before I reached Brewster Academy. I can remember being in sixth grade, soon after the cockpit incident. The rest of my class was engrossed in math problems. At that early age, I'd already learned to sit next to the Asian girls, as they knew all the answers. After I'd wasted pretty much the whole class writing punch lines, I realized I needed to attempt some work. I was leaning across and squinting so hard to see the answers of the Korean chick next to me, it looked as if I were making fun of her in a Hello Kitty sort of way. And I found this unbelievably funny. I just started laughing, and I couldn't stop. First, because I mistakenly looked like an enormous racist, and second, because I was the only person in the class, barring the teacher (and that wasn't a given), who would get the joke. They were fully immersed in their pointless activity while I was having fun. Joke's on Jew.

Coming hard on the heels of my pilot phase, it was a further revelation. Their conformity amused me. Why the fuck were they sweating over equations when they could be yukking it up? It made no sense to me.

The following summer I was sent away to camp. It wasn't officially a Jew-kid camp, but it certainly had those leanings. It was the "right" camp, the one considered correct to attend, which was a complete affront to me. Why the fuck would I want to go where everyone else was going? I had to deal with those dicks during the rest of the year; why would I want to sit around a campfire with them?

I had no interest in going, and once I was there, all I wanted to do was swiftly get kicked out and never invited back. The cool kids at the camp all played tennis; they represented the "alpha males." In an unspoken fashion, this was how the hierarchy was established, by the accuracy of your first serve. I couldn't play tennis. I hated tennis. To make my feelings clear, I decided to piss on the tennis court. Everyone saw me—it was during a match. It was probably the most subversive, blasphemous thing I could have done.

Campers and counselors alike were mortified. It was like I'd rectally probed someone with the camp's ornamental replica tomahawk. It wasn't subtle, but it helped do the job and taught me a valuable lesson. Yes, I could have spent hours trying to come up with the perfect, complicated scheme to bring about my release, but sometimes all you need to do is piss on the tennis court.

Incredibly, this wasn't a serious enough crime to immediately result in expulsion. It was more of a crime against their inherent beliefs than a chargeable offense. So they pinned a series of trash-can fires on me for good measure. I didn't set any fires—I wasn't a pyro. There were a lot of weird kids at that camp.

This mild level of delinquency and unhappiness continued until my parents were sick to death of me. They just wanted me out of the house and didn't really care how much it cost them. It cost them roughly $35,000 a year. Attendance at Brewster Academy was considered a privilege. It had to be at that price. But my parents and I knew I was being shipped off for the sake of their sanity and their standing in our hometown. I had started to attract attention, the bad sort of attention that I enjoyed. It was the very thing they fervently strived to avoid. All I had to do was not get thrown out of the joint. I managed to achieve this. Just.

When I got there, it was quite a shock. The guidebook was as thick as the yellow pages, with rules covering everything from eating to grooming. Every aspect of your life was regimented and scheduled. You ate, slept, and were educated at distinct times and couldn't beat off without a signed note from the nurse. I'd never been in an atmosphere as tightly controlled as this. The campus was beautiful, the kids were cruel, and the law was strictly enforced. Anything could be considered an altercation, and punishment was swift, vengeful, and often unfair. This was going to be a challenge. And behind it all was Doucheborn.

Doucheborn was the principal architect of the establishment's regimen, and he epitomized everything I'd grow to hate in the world and would become determined to eradicate. As I explained, he was "dean of students," but really he was the warden, and we were his inmates. He lived and died by the book. Which is why I took every page of the book, ripped it out, and wiped my ass with it—figuratively. Now I brand any example of small-minded wretchedness and people who possess his particular brand of charmlessness as "Doucheborn."

My first year there was entirely an operation in casing. I watched; I observed. I worked out how things ticked, where the weaknesses lay, who to target for maximum efficiency. I pored over the handbook as if it were a map leading to maximum disruption. I didn't socialize; I wasn't interested in forming friendships or forging bonds. I looked upon the whole experience as an exercise in how far I could push things before they fell over. It was the only way to stifle the boredom and disrupt the status quo. By the start of the next year I was ready to act. I started with my wardrobe. I transformed.

My nickname on campus soon became GQ. It wasn't necessarily a term of endearment. I wanted to look like something you'd see spread across that month's *Esquire*. I always abided by the specifications of the dress code but never indulged the spirit of it. You were required to wear a blazer, a shirt, a tie, khaki pants, sensible shoes. I wore all those things. They just happened to be the finest designer examples of them, purloined during holiday romps through Neiman Marcus.

Ferragamo, Zegna, Prada, Burberry—I dressed decades older than I was and always accessorized with Louis Vuitton. It wasn't preppie in the least, way more Madison Avenue with sleek, debonair lines. I wore Gucci shoes, even in the depths of winter when the snow was up to your ass. But I made my mark. I was noticed. The kids made fun of me. Good. I loved that attention, the negative attention. The authorities at the school hated my new look. They knew I was up to something; they just couldn't quite work out what it was. This was to be the model for my behavior during the next few years.

I now began to identify particular rules and devise ways to disable them. Why? Because that's what I excelled at. I was never going to make it onto the mathletics team or be the lacrosse captain. If that was your lot in life, good for you. But those people are completely designated into those roles. Every math wiz looks the same; every high school sports star acts the same. They really want to be recognized and lauded for that shit? But that was exactly what was expected of you. Do well in these rigidly narrow areas, and we'll give you a cheap trophy and a pat on the head. Excuse me if I don't perform backflips.

I had other ways to be recognized. My skills lay in self-promotion. It was like I was campaigning for a platform—and that platform was me. And like all politicians, I wanted people to notice me, to be entertained. It all became about performance, what could I do to provide maximum impact with minimal effort. I learned a massive amount in that first year. Not in class, of course, but about my particular talents and how to utilize them. I was born to subvert and manipulate. For the first time in my life, I was emerging as a role model. While many still despised me, a growing element started to notice and appreciate my efforts. I was totally unique, and if you're unique, you'll eventually get noticed. I was becoming a star. I honed my act over the coming months.

My Jewlosophy has always been to target the one thing you excel at and be the Tiger Woods, Lance Armstrong, and Mike Tyson of your field. OK, those are great bad examples, but I want to be on the highest part of the podium. You need to be the best of breed, the proprietary eponym. In my view, if Justin Ross Lee doesn't come up as the number one answer on *Family Feud* when the has-been host asks, "Who is the biggest asshole self-promoter in the world?" I have failed. So, at Brewster, I focused on what I was good at, which was bucking the system. The clothes and the fashion were just the hors d'oeuvres.

From Water Boy to Cable Guy

So the huge, glaring error that Doucheborn and Subaru Sue made, entirely instigated by me, was a by-product of my new water-boy status. They assumed I just adopted the lowly position to get out of doing gym, which was completely true. But there were more-damaging repercussions to their decision. You see, in order to distribute water to the athletes in my care, some form of transportation was required. I couldn't be expected to *carry* large amounts of water *on my back* like a *serf*. So the school provided a vehicle for the movement of the juice. They gave me a golf cart. The idiots.

As soon as the golf cart was in my possession, it never left my side. I'd drive it around campus, I'd drive it to class, I'd drive it into town, and I'd drive it in the snow and ice. I'd take it off-roading. It became well known to the local Wolfeboro Police Department, who continually fielded complaints from bystanders nearly mown down by my reckless driving. I'd take dates out in it; we'd go for beer runs or pick up pizzas. If there had been a drive-in nearby, I would have attended happily. I plagued my enemies with drive-by supersoakings. Pretty much the only place it didn't go was onto the soccer field during sporting events. I was never too interested in the "work" side of the job.

I soon became known and hated as the kid with the golf cart. They were all getting used to the fashion thing, so this new wrinkle was a helpful reminder of my presence. And once they started to get used to the golf cart, I knew I needed to develop that also. So I started to modify it.

It was a shoddy, white 1980s Yamaha G-1 golf cart with a flimsy plastic roof and unimaginative design. But as this conveyance was now a major weapon in my arsenal, it needed to reflect my personality. I adapted the roof and turned it into a convertible. Now everyone could see me coming. I'd scour the want ads and Internet for suitable accessories. Soon it was slathered in decals, upholstered in leather, and outfitted with chrome rims on the tiny wheels. And for a final definitive fuck-you, I sourced and bought an actual Mercedes symbol and added it to the front of the grill, the angle of which changed with each subsequent crash. Oh yeah, I crashed the fucking thing at least ten times. It's a miracle no one died. Probably because it could manage a top speed of about twelve miles per hour.

I avoided getting it taken away from me or getting kicked out completely by using a few of the manipulation strategies I had developed. I'd befriended the campus security guard, Charlie, whom everyone else treated like shit. I showed him total respect, because I knew he could help me. No one appreciated that Charlie was powerful. The same way valet parkers hold all the power wherever they work. They know where the bodies are buried. They see the sins of the managers. They appreciate how everything works. I quickly learned that the guy at the top of the tree wasn't important, but the guy who could get you what you want was. And Charlie was no different. He was happy to give me the heads up when I'd pushed things too far and the shit was about to hit the fan. He was a useful ally.

He'd provide me with keys to certain parts of the building usually off-limits to the likes of me. Information about possible raids and searches were slyly passed my way. Certain professors were secretly on my side, too (they probably enjoyed how much I tortured Doucheborn), so I'd get passing grades if necessary. Some of my work was plagiarized or outsourced. Why not? If I'd shown even the slightest scrap of individuality or personality, they'd fail me anyway. They just wanted the answers on the page and to be left the hell alone.

I was also hacking into the dean's e-mail, which helped me find out when things were getting peppery. Which was increasingly often. The golf cart was a great tool for getting me noticed, and it didn't break any rules. But elsewhere in academic life, I was slightly more controversial. There was shit that would have gotten me kicked out instantly if it was discovered.

I had a roommate. As some kind of cosmic joke, he was from Germany. He liked to remind me of that fact as often as he could, usually in relation to the actions of his people against mine during the war. Grim, I know, but this was typical boarding-school humor. He was an obnoxious prick, not in the artful way I was, but just in a dickish, teenage-boy way. He enjoyed lighting individual pubic hairs on fire in front of me so he could revel in the smell of burning hair. I once sprayed Lysol on the flame just as he was about to ignite one, and he fireballed like Michael Jackson on the set of a Pepsi commercial. Needless to say, he wasn't impressed. In fact, he beat the shit out of me, so I decided our time together must come to an end.

I'd already recognized the influence of the medical unit and how their manipulation was a powerful force. Getting a doctor's note for any number of conditions was easy, especially mental conditions. Look at the shit I did! Everyone was already calling me crazy; it wasn't hard to get it documented. These mental issues progressed until I developed a powerful case of sleepwalking—or at least that's what I told the campus nurse. I'd wake up in all sorts of crazy positions, sometimes with my hands around my roommate's throat. I mean, we could have risked it and hoped it just went away, but I would have hated for something terrible to happen to him. With a sigh, they agreed, and he was shipped off down the hall, and I was allowed a dorm room to myself. The only boarder to enjoy this luxury. Once I had the place to myself, I started to get really inventive with my indiscretions.

Now, I will fully admit, I was fairly delusional at this time. I was flying. I was dressed like Patrick Bateman, driving beautiful girls around the campus in my pimped-out golf cart and now had my own room to take them back to. I soon developed this full New York–penthouse fantasy and started to remodel my dorm room to resemble something Trump would be proud to reside in. I brought in my own furniture and fittings. I had a Clapper to turn the electrical devices on and off. There was a refrigerator, neon signs, and air-conditioning. Way more shit than any of the dorm parents had.

I had my own food brought in. I never ate in the cafeteria; I needed time alone in my room to devise the next ludicrous scheme. So I got very friendly with the local Chinese restaurant in Wolfeboro, which would deliver to me, sometimes several times a day, in all weathers. The owner would slap snow chains on his Honda Odyssey and head out to Brewster to deliver my lo mein. I was putting his fucking kids through college. When

I finally left school, I had MSG withdrawal sickness for a week. It was a pretty sweet setup but was missing a vital component.

Like all kids everywhere ever, I watched an inordinate amount of television growing up. So one of the strangest elements of boarding-school life was the sudden absence of in-room TV. It was completely prohibited. The faculty had it, obviously—they even had cable. I couldn't see why I should be deprived of the delights of *Seinfeld* and Jennifer Aniston just because the guidebook said so. There was no way I could splice and hook up an illegal cable line. But I knew some nerds who could.

I outsourced to the AV club, using a two-pronged attack of flattery and a light accusation, suggesting such a technical feat would be completely beyond them. Obviously this provoked the geeks into action to the point where they were *dying* to hook up my cable and prove their worth. They tapped into the dorm parent's supply and ran the wires across my ceiling and into a TV hidden under a box, just in case there was a sudden room search. They never caught me, or it. Not until I left and they found the whole setup during maintenance. I'm still proud of that.

So now I was the only kid on campus with a TV hookup. The notion that I'd fucked the rules so thoroughly was even more satisfying than night after night of illicit Letterman. It was risky and illegal. Discovery would mean immediate suspension. But I loved the excitement connected to this, the same buzz every criminal feels. Plus it had the added perk of attracting young ladies into my room, like slutty bees to honey.

"You wanna come over, watch *Sex and the City*, order Chinese food, play with my Clapper?" It never failed.

Legions of girls in my room was obviously pretty sweet, but to me, it was all about the game. Just winning in unconventional ways. Positive reinforcement through beating the system. Getting out of these manufactured obligations. Not having to do what other people had to do. The school had in place every system necessary for me to learn and destroy, everything I needed to subsequently survive in New York City society. It was such a concentrated microcosm, the perfect storm of self-help and self-instruction.

It was like a fortress of privilege, and I became a master of creatively breaking the rules, getting into trouble, and then figuring out a solution. The perfect grounding for life beyond central New Hampshire. Getting known for being hated. And they all fucking hated me. The faculty, the kids, the town. I looked like a Jewish Thurston Howell, didn't give a shit, completely manipulated all of them, and was banging the prettiest girl in school. Oh, didn't I mention that? Yes, the hottest girl in school was on my arm—and elsewhere.

Everyone wanted her. She was incredible. She appeared at least five or six years older than she was, looking completely indecent in dress code. The first time I spotted her I nearly totaled my golf cart. To this day I don't know how I pulled it off, but she was all mine.

She was to provide possibly the most important lesson I learned at that time. My tenure at Brewster Academy was finally coming to an end. The relief was palpable on all sides. From being this little sprat, scared of everything and daunted by the rules, to by the last year fucking owning the place. At least in my own mind. Everyone there knew who I was. Everyone. As I stood there at graduation, all I could think was "How the fuck did I get away with that?" There were some incredibly close calls, and the threat of military academy was dangled over me. Nonstop push-ups in a violently homoerotic atmosphere was not something I particularly desired. Perhaps the school didn't want to deal with the paperwork or my mother's hysterical crying jag that my expulsion would have initiated, but in any case they let me slide, and I stood there with the rest of my graduating class, wearing a goofy hat. I smiled at Doucheborn throughout the ceremony.

I was a legend when I split. The scars I left on the institution still remain to this day. While not mentioning me by name, the student handbook has been revised to reinforce the very rules I circumvented. So I escaped and headed off to college, feeling pretty cocky. I still had my hot high school girlfriend but let my guard down. Big mistake. Out of sight, out of mind, as they say, and she cheated on me pretty much the second Lake Winnipesaukee froze over. I was heartbroken but way the fuck wiser. That's what I learned. Don't let them forget you. You have to keep your profile up, or else you'll be miserable, alone, and embarking on an Olympic-scale blow habit.

What I Learned in Boarding School

- It's not what you know but who you know. Having a man on the inside is invaluable.
- If at first you don't succeed, outsource.
- If there's no law against it, then it's legal. Make them change the law if they want you to stop.
- There's nothing noble in overachieving. Overunderachieving is more impressive.
- Anything can be turned into a performance.
- Negative attention can turn into positive results.
- Invoke the power of the euphemism. I could never be a water boy, but director of student athletics was something I could live with.
- Embarrassment can stop you doing a lot of fun things.
- You have to reinvent to be remembered.
- No one gives a shit what you did in high school.

Lesson 2: Circumventing the Circumcision

The fucking nerve. The fucking nerve of looking at me and saying, "Here's your little box. Hop in, and keep your trap shut." As
if that could possibly apply to me.

But that's what I was facing, growing up in Scarsdale, New
York. It was as regimented and defined as the Indian caste
system, but with BMWs instead of *tuk-tuks*. Despite the huge
amount of money and privilege sloshing around, no one had
any freedom, with everyone pinned down by this fear of being
considered "different." Your status was defined by your perceived successes.

"My daughter won the spelling bee."

"My son scored the winning home run."

Who gives a shit? Get to the back of the tremendously long
line of everyone else who has done that. When I was young,
I didn't know what I wanted to do; I just knew I didn't want
that. I didn't want anyone pointing at me and saying, "Here's
what you're going to be." Firstly, I didn't think any of these people were in a position to dictate. They didn't seem so happy
to me—it appeared as if they constantly lived their lives in
fear of not living up to each other. Secondly, I knew the roles
being offered weren't for me. Having letters after your name
impressed characters like my mother, which is exactly why I
had no interest in pursuing any of those things.

It became a defining tenet of my life, circumventing the
circumcision. And this has nothing to do with the biblical.
I'm not saying you should do anything in particular with your
foreskin, either pro or anti. Lop it off, sew it back on, have it
pierced—I don't give a shit as long as I don't have to see it. I'm
talking about embarking on an alternative rite of passage.

My mother can't even say "Jew" out loud, for Christ's sake.
She covers her mouth and whispers the word. It's adorably

hilarious. She's convinced that anyone in the retail or liveried transportation industries who hears about our religious inclinations is going to either jack up the price, blow us up, or spit in our entrees. We'd already been transformed from the Liebowitzes to the Lees by my great-grandfather, who wanted to get into showbiz. The die was cast. We were to be "quiet Jews" like the other Jews of Scarsdale. Just Jewish enough to represent but not be noticed.

Again, I hated the idea that I had to suppress my heritage or present it in an "acceptable" way. So I became a "Super Jew," as the *New York Post* delights in calling me. It drives my family crazy, but I'm determined to circumvent the circumcision.

"Justin, can't you cut out all the Jewish stuff?" my dad demands every time I see him. You see, we worked very hard to get accepted as Lees, and suddenly I'm dragging us back down into the last century.

This is the same guy who wanted me to become an investment banker. No, he demanded that I become an investment banker. Can you imagine walking into an office building, carrying a bag with a big dollar sign on it, and handing it over to me? I'd go on shopping sprees for shiksas. What a fucking joke.

No, I figured out pretty quickly that these predetermined paths ascribed to you led directly to an ugly wife, fat kids, and a gut full of misery. You need to run kicking and screaming in the opposite direction of that train wreck.

There seems to be some weird shame attached to nonconformity. As if you're letting someone down if you don't do exactly what was expected of you. Who are you letting down for fuck's sake? Jesus? Buddha? Your parents? They'll be long dead while you're still trudging to the same soul-destroying nine-to-five.

Why excel at mediocrity? There are plenty of people doing that already. Consider your talents, figure out what gets you wet or hard, and strive to focus on that. And if you piss people off along the way, then you're obviously doing something right.

CHAPTER 3

CON-UKKAH! GETTING AWAY WITH ANYTHING

The judge, in my opinion, looked remarkably like a scrotum. An angry, elderly scrotum with a thin, pubish beard that failed to help the whole scrotal resemblance. This prick surveyed his courtroom and the motley collection of filth, degenerates, and subpar Mass Pike hookers that make up a decent proportion of the greater Boston metropolitan area and looked as if someone had just placed a shitty dick atop his gavel.

Front and center, standing amongst these dregs, was my good self. I was dressed to the nines. My sartorial game was on point, Ralph Lauren himself may have considered my ensemble "a little too much." Smooth, coiffured, pressed, exuding privilege and good breeding. I epitomized affluence and the obvious, God-given expectation that I deserved a different tier of justice than the sickening collection of excreta currently cluttering up my eyeline.

Obviously I felt far superior to my courtmates. And in the eyes of the law I was also superior. Just not in a good way. I was the ringleader of these delinquents. I had instigated and then evolved into the head rabble-rouser of a mildly disruptive incident that snowballed into a serious fracas and finally blew up into a full-scale, citywide riot. And not only were there eye-witnesses and circumstantial evidence to attest to my guilt; the entire melee had been filmed and then uploaded to a brand new video-hosting site, something called YouTube. One day YouTube would be a powerful tool in my social-crime arsenal. At this moment, it was being used as evidence to support a felonious charge.

The infamous footage was almost comical in its guilt-de-fining attributes. I was standing on the hood of a car, holding a powerful industrial megaphone, bellowing at a group of obe-sely huge Northeastern linebackers, "Hey, losers, I know you can't win a football game, but can you tip that Toyota Celica over?" while the surrounding throng chanted, "Justin Lee! Jus-tin Lee! Justin Lee!" like I was the Al Sharpton of this scene. Then the camera zoomed in on my face and framed all my identifying characteristics perfectly.

All that was missing was my social security number and dick size flashing across the bottom of the fucking screen. As usual, I found myself in this criminally compromising position due to a number of consecutive events spiraling dangerously out of control. The Patriots had just won the World Series, or the Celtics had just won the Stanley Cup. Some shit like that. I'm a Jew with a Chinese name, so sports are not really my forte. But when I looked out my dorm-room window and saw a drunk, aggressive street party taking place, celebrating this steroid-induced victory, I saw an opportunity. These people needed leadership. A Moses. A Maccabee. A crooked cantor to funnel their violent tendencies in a more creative direction. And, obviously, I was the perfect candidate for the role.

Did all of this get ever so slightly out of hand? Certainly. Did I participate in this madness? It can't be denied. Did I know that my hectoring would be the trigger for one of Boston's worst sports-related riots? Of course not. The thought might have excited me, but I never dreamed I could be responsible for such wanton destruction. Once I had invigorated the crowd and various vehicles were happily burning, I retreated back to my room and merrily listened to the mayhem outside at a safe distance. It wasn't until the next morning when two Boston cops interrupted my hangover to tell me I was being charged with felony inciting of a riot, malicious destruction of property, and public intoxication that I realized I had significantly fucked up. They made it very clear that I was to be made an example of. It turns out cops don't like riots. Who knew? I was going to jail.

Which was why I was now standing before this slightly scrotal judge, dressed like Jay Gatsby, manically trying to get him to notice the contrast between me and everyone else who stepped foot in this courtroom. But the gentleman would not be swayed. He might have been surprised to see me moving in the same circles as Boston's leading filth and riot participants (why we were all being tried together was completely beyond me), but he surmised that I was the only one with the mental prowess to dictate such well-orchestrated civil disobedience and so deemed me their supreme leader. And he was right.

After broadcasting the entertaining, if life-destroying, footage to the court, there was testimony from a succession of shell-shocked local residents, emotionally scarred small-business owners, and the titleholder of the afflicted car, who sobbed like a pregnant prom queen at thoughts of his poor Celica.

Throughout this litigation, the judge looked faintly nauseated. Eventually he turned to me and asked if I had anything to say.

This was it. My time to shine. Fortunately, I was prepared. I knew that my ass was on the line. Literally. If I fucked this up, my derriere would be the next afternoon activity for the residents of D Wing to enjoy. I attempted to channel all the disgraced miscreants I could—Eliot Spitzer, Bill Clinton, OJ—and addressed the judge with a facial expression usually exhibited by televangelists caught *shtupping* Hooters waitresses and now trying to make amends.

"Your Honor," I began, possibly bowing a little. "Like you and the rest of these fine, upstanding citizens [humble nod] I was appalled, nay sickened, by what I witnessed in that hideous video footage [angry fist slam]. I did not recognize that individual in the video. That individual was not me [baleful stare]. That person, standing on the hood of that burning Toyota and screaming obscenities through an American bullhorn [puffs out chest with patriotic pride] was a different human being than the one before you now [holds hands in prayer-like gesture]. I am thoroughly ashamed of my actions that day [wipes away tear]. It would be so easy to blame the pain medication I was taking for an injury caused while helping a woman change a flat tire by the freeway in the snow. But I only have myself to blame. I have disgraced my family [swallows]. I have disgraced my noble seat of learning [voice cracks a little]. I have disgraced this magnificent city that has been so welcoming to me in so many ways [smiles angelically]. And, most of all, I have disgraced myself [bows head]. After much soul-searching and lengthy discussions with various counselors and religious leaders [attempts to look less "Jewy"], I have decided that my greatest wish is to give back to the community that I have so maliciously maligned. I can only hope that in your wise and special heart [opens eyes wide] your honor can allow me to compensate for my vicious misdeeds in an appropriate and restitutional fashion [stares at floor with sorrow]."

The judge sighed heavily. "And what do you suggest, Mr. Lee?"

My lip quivered in thought. "After a great deal of research and meetings with nonprofit organizations, I feel the greatest use of my talents would be to work with a group that helps the hardest hit amongst us. One of my great role models is former president Jimmy Carter, whom I respect for his unwavering faith and charitable approach to life. It would be an honor, Your Honor, if I was able to work alongside this great man, in spirit at least, and volunteer to assist Habitat for Humanity."

"Fine. Two hundred fifty hours' community service."

My fancy, high-powered lawyer bartered it down to 125. And that's how I got a free vacation to Brazil out of a Boston circuit judge.

***

Minutes after arriving at Northeastern University, I was already in a slight state of panic. It was the heady brew of having a whole new toy box to play with, but also realizing the vastness of the place. I'd completely conquered my prep school, to the point where the general behavioral guidelines had to be completely rewritten after I left to reflect my various ridiculous misdeeds. But this was completely different. Rather than a few hundred kids, there were thousands, and getting their attention was going to be tricky.

My first minor victory was easy. By pulling the same shit that I had at Brewster, I'd managed to swing a single dorm room for myself. I'd claimed to be agoraphobic or claustrophobic or a projectile bed wetter or some shit. I can't remember. But whatever it was, it worked, and I found myself with a tiny but sweet spot all to myself. Once in this esteemed position, I started a period of casing. I just sat back and watched. I needed an angle. Something to weasel my way in with the alumni and make a name for myself.

Oh, and I occasionally studied. I think the official name of my major was "Entrepreneurship." It was as bullshitty as it sounds. It was selected solely on the basis of a simple equation: the amount of energy I would have to expend on attendance multiplied by the amount of shit I could get away with. Listen, there is one rule for any student attending higher education: if you're working hard to get that fucking scroll and stupid hat after four years, you are a dumbass. A massive dumbass. No one needs to work hard at college. It's not designed for work and perseverance. You're paying a fucking fortune to be within those walls—they honestly expect you to sweat as well? If you find yourself applying yourself to anything other than drinking and pussy and general indolence during your university tenure, stop and get a job at Jiffy Lube. You're in the wrong place. Like most things, it was a question of working smarter, not working hard. And, with college, you don't even have to work that smart. Befriend your tutor so he knows your name, make sure he sees you on occasion, and buy or steal the coursework from someone smarter than you. Simple.

So I had snuck into this bullshit course that I barely attended. But within the confines of Stetson West, my coed dorm that was filled with hundreds of fellow undergrads, I was a fucking plebeian. I needed to be loved. And the fastest way to obtain love? You buy it. And I had the perfect way to achieve this.

Soon after arriving in Boston, I'd befriended a Haitian cab driver called Mr. Rock. And this fucker loved me. Can you imagine how shitty it is being a Haitian cab driver in Boston? How many Irish dickholes you have to deal with on a daily basis? All I had to do was show Mr. Rock the merest sliver of respect, and he was willing to do any fucking thing for me. His loyal Crown Victoria became my personal limousine, available at any time of the day or night. I'd just make a quick phone call, and he'd ditch whatever fare he was ferrying and come and get me. Then we'd go and pick up a couple of quarts of good Haitian rum and shoot the shit for a few hours.

Remember, I was barely eighteen at this point. And unlike New Hampshire, Boston appeared to give a shit about underage drinking. I considered this to be the ideal access point to gain the attention and respect of my student brethren. By getting them good and drunk. Justin Lee had arrived in Massachusetts, and he would be recognized.

But there was a small, if nagging, problem. I was surrounded by assholes. The pricks in my dorm were happy to partake of my illegally obtained rum or any other liquor I could supply via Mr. Rock, but they didn't give a shit about me. I was just the chump provisioning booze, and once the drink ran out they dropped me like a hot latke. This kind of maneuver may have worked with the kids back at Brewster Academy, but if I wanted to run with the big dogs, or at least convince the big dogs how great I was, I'd need to think of something trickier.

Luckily, I had a near neighbor in the dorms who was utterly fucking corrupt. It turned out he had the skills, equipment, and motivation to make fake IDs. But he lacked the sales prowess to turn these little plastic rectangles into a gold mine. We went into business together. He'd churn out the merchandise, and I would find us prospective customers. I figured that rather than simply handing out free booze just like that guy—wait, what was his name? Oh yeah, Jesus. Rather than handing out free booze like that hippy, if I could provide a resource that guaranteed unlimited booze to the holder of the illegal identification, I'd soon be catapulted to campus hero status.

Of course, there was a slight catch. The entire legal system. Since those dicks had driven planes into various high-profile buildings and a completely innocent Pennsylvanian field, officialdom didn't look too kindly on any sort of fake identification. In fact, it was a felony in Massachusetts to make and distribute this sort of stuff. Even if it was only to college kids looking to buy a case of Mad Dog, if we got busted doing this, it would mean serious shit. But I thought it was worth rolling the dice to make a little bit of a splash in this new environment.

So we whipped up a batch of the contraband—and they looked beautiful. Sure, if you flipped them over, you'd discover they were on the back of an expired Blockbuster Video card and they lacked a hologram or an official stamp, but any short-sighted or lazy or slightly backward liquor-store clerk would almost certainly be taken in. With a bit of luck. But before we could start distribution, we needed to test the stuff. And as I was the charismatic one in the partnership, it was up to me to see if these fucking things flew.

I selected a pretty-bland-looking bodega that was far enough away from campus that I wouldn't be instantly branded as a dumb Northeastern student trying to buy booze illegally with a crappy fake ID. I dressed like an adult and selected a bottle of wine. A good bottle of wine. A thirty-dollar bottle of wine. Just one. And no small talk. No nervous babbling about the weather or sports or the knockers on that chick in the parking lot. I picked a classy beverage, dropped it on the counter, and instantly reached for my ID. I didn't wait to be asked. I was wise to the protocol and knew what needed to happen.

But this guy, shit, I don't know what happened, but he was onto me. Maybe it was a problem in the bedroom at home. Maybe the owner had just chewed his ass out for selling to underage delinquents. Maybe he remembered that he was a shit-poor clerk in the butt end of Boston, and I was some privileged jackass buying fancy wine he could never hope to understand or enjoy and I probably had some hot, rich bitch in my Beemer outside that I was getting ready to poke. I don't know the reasons, but this asshole wasn't buying it. Something didn't add up, and he got all *CSI* on my ass.

But he was sneaky. He didn't throw the fucking thing back over the counter at me or laugh in my face or instantly call the Feds. He asked for a second piece of ID.

"Store policy," he said.

And this is where I truly fucked up. At that point I should have made my excuses and left. "Oh, my other ID is out in the car"—that kind of shit. But instead, like the fucking wet-dicked, naive infant that I was, I panicked and handed him my college ID. My real, legitimate Northeastern ID. What the god-damned hell was I thinking? As well as instantly placing me in the wrong age range, it also provided this douche bag with all my contact details.

He looked at it, looked at me, looked back at it, and then said the fateful words: "Something isn't right here."

Then he reached for the phone.

Of course I did what every true, red-blooded American would do in that situation. I ran. I bolted the fuck out of there and didn't stop until I was back in my room. The cops arrived a couple of hours later. At first I pretended I wasn't there. This just pissed them off further. So eventually I opened the door to two Suffolk County deputies who, like most law enforcement officials, hated me instantly.

"What took you so long?" I asked.

To their credit, they didn't drag me through the dorm and bang me up overnight. I could have gotten arrested. I actually think my stupidity saved me. They knew that some big coun-terfeiting mover and shaker wouldn't be so dumb as to use their college ID alongside their fake one. They gave me a "notice to appear," which meant I'd be heading to court.

Luckily, for me, the law is completely biased in favor of rich, disgusting, white assholes like myself. I don't know if you realized that. Hey, I don't make the rules. The worst thing I had to face was breaking the news to my family, and after a few hours of anxious Jewish whining and disappointed berating, they provided me with a decent lawyer and a game plan.

First, I had to talk to the detectives assigned to my case and go over all the details of the incident before we all went to see the judge. Incredibly, even though these people are trained to detect bullshit from two towns over, I completely bullshitted them. I gave them the vaguest descriptions of the people I claimed to have gotten the merchandise from (I never ratted out my coconspirator; even I have some values), saying one was black, one was white. Youngish, colorful clothing, sneakers. That kind of crap. And they ate it up. They jotted it all down and even thanked me for my cooperation! If nothing else came out of this miserable business, I was proud of the fact that I had completely bamboozled a couple of veteran cops who totally ate up the lies I was sending their way. The lesson learned here: some cops aren't that smart. Highly dangerous, but not that smart.

So I got dragged to court. There was a slap on the wrist and no record. My lies to the detectives convinced the judge that I was just a dumb teen after some cheap hootch, not a felony-level manufacturer of false IDs. They believed that I was just an idiot who got out of his depth. Which, frankly, I was. There might have been a small fine or something, but basically I got away with it.

Yeah, I was learning a lot. Not in the realms of entre-preneurship (obviously) but life lessons in how not to direct my college career. I had swung and struck out. My booze connections via Mr. Rock and my fledgling criminal career had both ended in ignominy. I decided to do something so completely against my own nature, it sickens me to think about it. It was a combination of desperation and sheer panic. I was ready to try anything, and I really went left field. I decided to go legit. Biggest mistake of my fucking life. Listen to me, this is important: never go legit. Never try to curry favor by traditional, well-established means. It is always doomed to failure. I had to learn the hard way. Don't make the same mistake I did.

So how did I decide to win over the denizens of Stetson West? To get them to respect me and become their god? I ran for dorm president. Now, you might be asking, "What the fuck is dorm president?" I honestly don't know. But I thought it might provide a toehold in the social standing of the dipshits living around me. As you can imagine, entering a popularity contest is a terrible way to gain popularity. I was instantly branded a dweeb, a cock-knuckle, and a grasping, terrible tool. All monikers I completely deserved. Once I was in office, I would have the position and prestige to fuck things up from the inside. Was I deluded? Of course! I was eighteen! Have you ever tried to talk to an eighteen-year-old? Unless they're female, Swedish, and boneable, it's really not worth it.

But for once, luck was on my side. Unsurprisingly, no other idiot wanted the fucking job, so I was the only asshole on the ballot. The only one. Perhaps this lack of competition should have tipped me off to the quality of the gig. But at least I was guaranteed to win.

But then the bitch stepped in.

Who was the bitch? Fuck knows. Some twat who decided to fuck with me for her own despicable reasons and whose name I have subsequently suppressed into invisibility. But this bitch decided it would be hilarious to make herself a last-minute write-in candidate. The day of the vote she suddenly rolled up, shoved her tits in the faces of a few freshmen, squealed "Vote for me," and fucking won. I was the only name on the ballot, and I lost. As elections go, this one was not exactly an ego boost.

I'd been completely humiliated, and rather than being the elected king of Stetson West, I was a fucking laughingstock. The prick who had run uncontested and lost. So this was the state of mind I was in when the great Super Bowl riot took place—crushed, defeated, and out of ideas. My lowly position amongst my peers had actually dropped lower. Which was one of the mitigating factors in channeling this confusion and rage toward those footballing pituitary cases full of malt liquor and misplaced bravado. And if the disastrous election had given me one thing, it was a powerful megaphone that I could now use to provoke the delinquents down on the street into violent, antisocial behavior.

So yeah, I fucked up. My actions did indeed make me a legend at Northeastern. I was the riot guy. If I hadn't been instantly suspended, I might have gotten the occasional high five. And thanks to my ill-judged fake-ID scam, my name was known to the local authorities and I was looking at a serious offense. Again I had to crawl to Daddy and demand legal assistance or drag the family name through the mud. And once the judicial wheels were in motion, I tried to find a way of turning the whole shitty mess to my advantage. My defense team convinced me that community service was the best result we could expect, but there was no way I was going to be picking up trash alongside I-93 in an ill-fitting orange jumpsuit next to a crack whore. That was inconceivable.

I knew there must be a way to serve my time and get a tan while I was doing it. That's when I came across Habitat for Humanity. In addition to honorably providing roofs to the toothless and the red of neck, they also had a few international projects, including one that was about to start in Brazil.

Brazil. Fucking Brazil.

One thing I knew: Brazil was warm and far away. I could sign up for a tour of duty so the court would be satisfied I was serving my sentence, and the charity would think I was some sort of decent human being. It was win-win. By liberally lying to all parties concerned, I was soon on a plane heading south. (I was nearly arrested during the flight, which you'll hear all about when JewJetting is discussed). After two flights, a bus ride, and possibly a passage on a fucking donkey (the details are hazy), I arrived in a small village somewhere around Juazeiro do Norte, which, roughly translated from the Portuguese, means "the middle of fucking nowhere." The locals had never seen a white face before. I was far away from home, in a completely alien place, waiting to get busted for my litany of lies at any second. And you know what? I had a fucking blast.

Look, I was surrounded by good-natured volunteers who didn't know what a monster I was. We could drink and eat for practically nothing. Obviously I soon ascended to the role of project supervisor (self-appointed), so I'd work on my tan while I watched Gentiles nail walls together and counted down the hours until I was free. I considered sending the scrotal judge a postcard, featuring me on a sun-kissed beach, a parrot on my shoulder, and a caption reading, "Really enjoying my community service! Thanks!" But I thought better of it.

The fucking balls on me, right? Rather than being sexually assaulted in a Massachusetts penitentiary, I was sipping caipirinhas. I mean, that has to be recognized as some kind of achievement. All I had to do was get a note detailing the hours I'd worked on official Habitat for Humanity letterhead, and I'd be in the clear. And of course, as these were decent, God-fearing people, they obliged. I served my time and I survived.

But, inevitably, there were repercussions. That was the end of my tenure at Northeastern University. I was kicked out for creating widespread havoc and general fuckupery. And after a painful meeting where I had to explain myself and my rather unusual expulsion record while pledging myself to good behavior, I was accepted by the University of Hartford. This was my safety school, my fallback position, my plan B. I decided I wasn't going to fuck up.

Well, let me clarify that. I decided I wasn't going to fuck up on campus. Officially, as a University of Hartford student, I would be squeaky clean. Keep my head down and do as little work as possible to achieve a passing grade. But outside the grounds of the delightful Connecticut educational establishment, I lived the life of a hellion.

First, I bagged a remarkable apartment in Hartford. I know that doesn't sound impressive, but this place was an absolute pussy moistener. Up on the twenty-sixth floor, which in that particular part of New England was like the eightieth floor. Decked the whole place out like the Playboy Club, but without the inherent fear of hepatitis and sexual assault from Hugh Hefner. Perhaps it was the influence of this swinging pad, or perhaps it was because there was absolutely nothing else to do within a hundred miles, but I started to frequent the local Indian-reservation casinos. I'd drive my Audi S4 at some ludicrous speed to Foxwoods or Mohegan Sun and drop a grand on blackjack or craps and then speed back downtown.

I basically thought I was Sam Rothstein. I befriended the local nightlife bigwigs in Hartford (they do exist) so I never had to pay for a drink (not that I could anyway—I was still underage). So I was gambling like a teenage Arab sheikh, banging cocktail waitresses, staying up until dawn at some glitzy hostelry, and eventually crashing in my high-rise bachelor pad. Oh, and occasionally making an appearance at school. But I didn't worry about that too much. My off-campus education was far more beneficial to my later life.

It was a pretty sweet situation, which I obviously had to fuck up. What's the overarching factor that you associate with late nights, gambling, fast cars, and general douchery? That's right: I developed a staggering coke habit. I mean, a respectable one. Blow became a significant accessory to my life. I'd never leave the house without it: keys, shades, fake ID, beautiful vial of coke.

I turned into the quintessential cocaine asshole. All my friends were coke friends. All the girls I fucked were coke girls. I was a sweating, burbling skeleton. For the first time since my infancy, I was starting to look like shit. I don't look good when I'm underweight. My face gets thin; my collarbones start to resemble oversized chew toys.

What I needed was a wake-up call. And I got one that resembled a crack whore blowing a tuba in my ear after an unfortunate one-night stand. I was deep into the depths of my coke phase. I was shit bored and headed to the casino. I hopped in the Audi, did a line off the steering column, and drove 130 miles per hour up to the front door. I immediately lost a grand on a bullshit hand of blackjack. I got royally annoyed, started to shout at the staff, and was quietly asked to leave.

I hopped back into the Audi. Hit 140 miles per hour on the highway home. Still had a nice full bag of coke in my pocket and was feeling pretty invincible. My Valentine 1 told me there were no cops on the road. Just green lights all the way.

Then the fucking blue lights hit my rearview mirror, and my dick went soft.

You sober up pretty fast when you realize you have an eight ball of cocaine on your person, you're drunk, your $500 radar detector malfunctioned, and you've just been moving faster than Dale Earnhardt Jr. with a firecracker in his rectum.

I couldn't throw the shit out the window—it was too late for that. I was suddenly pulled over on the side of the road, and a Connecticut state trooper was moving toward me. Fast. And he didn't look too cheery.

I had a brain wave. I don't know where it came from, whether divine intervention or my own delicious brain suddenly firing into action, but I started to act automatically. I reached under my seat and pulled out a shit cell phone I'd left in the car. It was a burner I'd taken to Brazil to beg for bail or ransom if anything had fucked up down there. It had a tiny amount of battery. The gods, or whatever higher power looks after ridiculous shits like me, were smiling. I dialed 911 and blurted out, "I just heard shots fired on Route 2 at exit 12, and I think there's an officer involved."

Then I hung up and dropped the phone just as the cop battered on my window with fury.

"License and registration right now!" he screamed at me. I handed them over, and he walked back to his vehicle. He was there for a second, then ran, *ran* back to me. He gave me back the documentation.

"I have another emergency. Consider yourself really fucking blessed," he spat at me, and waddled back to his car and sped away, siren blaring.

Look, I figured if I got busted, calling in a fake 911 report taking place at the next exit along wouldn't mean shit compared to possession of coke and driving under the influence. I would be in bad-boy jail. Not the prissy, white-collar place reserved for privileged pricks like me. I drove home at fourteen miles an hour with my asshole the size of a pinhead.

Even for me, that was an inspired combination of brilliance and lunacy. I don't know where that survival instinct came from, but thank fuck it kicked in when it did.

That was it. Shit was too scary. I stopped taking coke. I just stopped. I ditched my coke friends. And I decided to keep my head down for a while. Because I liked my asshole way too much.

Bending the Law, Breaking the Rules

I don't want to go to prison. I don't look good in orange. I don't even want to go to Lisbon, just because it sounds slightly like "prison." I wouldn't survive. Actually, scratch that, of course I'd survive. I'm JRL. I'd be running the block before the end of my first week. I'd have the warden on my knee and be betrothed to a beautiful transsexual Filipino called Cookie.

I'd just rather not, that's all. I like champagne and pussy and being outside. Three things that are quite marginal in most correctional facilities. Thankfully, these legal run-ins during my formative years made me realize the importance of lines. And I'm not talking about big, fat, tasty lines of blow. I mean the line between normal and criminal behavior that you can bend as much as is physically possible but that shouldn't be breached under any circumstances.

Look at it this way. You're walking along the corridor of some pointlessly lavish hotel that you've just paid $740 to sleep in for the night. You need soap. There's an unmanned maid's cart. The soap is right there. Nice soap. That L'Occitane shit or something. So you take one. No big deal. Then you think, "Wait, I'm a filthy fucker. I'm sure to need more soap than that." So you take four. Still no big deal. Then you think, "Hey, I paid good money to stay in this place, and they treated me like shit. There was a *USA Today* outside my fucking door, for fuck's sake. I deserve more." So you take twenty soaps. Are you ready to call the Feds yet? No, of course not.

So how many is too many? Is there a number? Is there a line? Sure, if you're not even a guest at the establishment and you crack a security guard over the head before cleaning the place out of their toiletries. Then you're a felon and deserve to go to jail. So the line does exist between those two places. And that's the gray area I love to play in.

I'd never swipe someone's wallet or hold up a Hess station. It's against my moral code. But I am fascinated by all forms of social crime—where there are victims and confusion and red faces, but no actual law is ever broken. Sure, you bend that line until it starts to make a worrying creaking sound. But you have to pull back before you follow through.

So my relationship with the law is complicated. You definitely want cops on your side. Or if not on your side, then miles and miles behind you. But you don't want to piss them off too severely.

Going to court thoroughly sucks. You have to get up really early, sit in a corridor with a bunch of people in soiled leisure wear, and have conversations with lawyers. Then policemen make you feel bad, your victims make you feel bad, and finally the judge makes you feel bad. There is simply no fun to be had within a million miles of this situation. But it took me two fairly severe court appearances, a spell of community service, and being a pussy hair away from a full felony cocaine-possession bust to realize that.

It was good to get all this shit out of the way. By the time I was ready for my first legitimate ID, I'd lived a life of recidivism and come out the other side. I knew I wanted to fuck shit up, but without any legal consequences. And I was on the road to working out exactly how to do that. The road to JRL.

CHAPTER 4

CELEBRITIES ARE MY CURRENCY

So things were looking truly fucking bleak for me. Not only had I lost my first job, but the fairly brutal way in which I had been dishonorably discharged made me realize that I had no business in business. Not in anybody else's business, anyway. The only thing that I completely excelled at was being me. But I couldn't imagine anyone planning to cut me a check for excelling at being me in the immediate future. I was broke. I was depressed. I was distressed. Trouble was He-brewing.

But desperation can often provide a great source of energy. I knew there was something there. All the limbs, vital organs, and discarded genitals needed to form the Manhattan Monster that would become JRL were hovering around me. I just needed to slot the pieces together. I had unchartable levels of charm, and a perverse skill for performing social crime. The incident at Pastis felt so right. The rush I experienced by displaying such public bullshit bravado was the ultimate high.

If I could just make a living by doing shit like that, I'd be pretty fucking happy. *Jewbilant*, if you will. But right now that seemed like an impossible dream, and I was flailing. And by flailing I mean sitting in my apartment, pouring vodka on my Honey Nut Cheerios.

I knew I needed to tear down the old me and rebuild. Begin some bullshit—maybe Jimmy Carter–style? Habitat for Humanity? I could always provide a safe space for derelicts to smoke meth in. But no, I needed to construct the legend of JRL. Generate that buzz again and share it with the world. Get my face out there. Be seen as someone. By everyone. Become as legitimate as any other schmuck haunting Page Six in the *New York Post* every single day.

The particular Page Six I was staring at was talking about a lavish launch party for the TV show *Entourage*, taking place that very evening. It was *a sign*. In terms of social crime, this could be the perfect hit for me right now. Exactly dead-on at the very beating heart of my demographic.

Just thinking about it gave me a warm, fuzzy feeling in my balls—and beyond. To suavely slip myself into that Hollywood soiree was exactly the sort of boost I needed. It wouldn't be easy, of course. I needed an accomplice. Or rather—since my accomplice would have no fucking idea what the fuck was going on—I needed a bimbo.

Her name wasn't actually Bimbo. As I am a gentleman, I shall not reveal this young lady's real name. Suffice it to say that she was a blonde with big tits. Really big tits. And I was desperate to get into her pants. Or she was desperate to get into mine. I can't quite remember now. Probably the latter.

I knew an HBO party was going to be a star-studded fest— it's that sort of show—and a glorious blonde on my arm would be the perfect prop. And that's entirely what I thought of her as: a prop. With tits. In fact, the tits were the prop. I figured I could get up to pretty much anything under the cover of that insanely beguiling rack. Should I find myself in real trouble, I could just shove her abundant chest toward the problem and run like hell.

She couldn't know what was going to go down. Actually, I had no idea what was going to happen myself, so there really wasn't anything to tell. I thought of her as a kind of drug mule, albeit a very attractive one. She was trafficking me into the party, but if she knew about the precious cargo she had concealed in her keister (figuratively, for now; physically, if I was lucky), it would be written all over her face. So no, no explanations as to her role. As far as the bimbo was concerned, she was getting a free ride into a swanky celebrity-filled shindig. That's what I wanted her to think. She thought she was using me to obtain free fizz and be within panting distance of Marky Mark. This is the essence of JRLism. Convince the suckers that they are getting something from me, when in fact I'm using them up the *tuchus*.

My plan, as far as I had one, was to get in, get pictures with every notable in attendance, and get out. To do that as a lone schlub would be difficult, bordering on pathetic. But with Tits McGee by my side, turning heads and manufacturing pant tents, life would be oh so much easier.

I called her and convinced her to meet me at my apartment. Why? I wanted to get pictures of her in my building. I was constructing a narrative of the entire evening, which I would spell out via images on my newly formed Facebook page. Placing her at my place added to the legitimacy of the event and also included a dash of intrigue. It suggested we were fucking or had fucked or were about to fuck. (There always needs to be a little romance in every story.)

Though I had yet to develop and solidify all my prime JRL manipulation techniques, I knew I had to be there early. If you plan to show up at something you are expressly not invited to, this is always the best option. Especially when famous people are involved. Most celebs aren't starved for parties. Even at events that are purportedly honoring them, the stars just want to show up, shake some hands, roll their eyes, and get the fuck out of there. The longer a celeb inhabits any fixed environment, the greater the chance some no-name will try to shove a spec script into the waistband of his Armani.

To wit, I had no desire to arrive hopelessly late and be refused entry into a party that famous people had already left and that thereafter was only populated by the sweaty, drunken production assistants.

The event in question was taking place at a swanky nightclub on Manhattan's West Side. One of those unnaturally cavernous establishments that have exclusive spaces within exclusive areas, which no one ever seemed to be exclusive enough to gain admittance to. Such clubs often possess a single obtuse name that is a mishmash of upper- and lowercase letters in an undecipherable font. Or they have no name at all. Viewed from the street, these places tend to show only a rolltop shutter on a derelict wall connected to a building that looks like a rug warehouse.

Not to brag—OK, I'll brag: I was looking fucking incredible. Every inch of me was impeccable. And my date complemented me perfectly: blond, glamorous, slightly disheveled, slightly wild in that way that men find irresistible. Even if we were going to completely flame out (and there was a good chance we would, since I had no idea what I was doing), we'd look magnificent while doing it. And I knew there'd be no half measures with this job. Either we were getting in or I was going home alone with a hard-on for company.

We arrived early. Stupidly early. My companion was baffled by this, so I fed her some bullshit about "screening times" and "fire codes" and "insulin injections," all of which she accepted in a clueless sort of way.

I hadn't completely scoped out just how enormous this event was going to be until we pulled up outside. I saw searchlights and banners and security and enough velvet ropes to supply a full-scale, decadent bondage party. HBO had pulled out all the fucking stops for this extravaganza. Shit. That didn't exactly make things easier for me and blondie. But because we were so early, there was just a rookie on the door. I deployed my secret weapon, and she deployed her less-than-secret weapons, aimed them at the dude, and smiled widely while I slipped in beside her. He was dazzled. We were in. It was that easy.

And there was that rush again.

I saw a steady stream of harassed-looking, white-shirted entities entering and leaving the main room, relishing their final few moments of palpable humanity before they were forced to offer champagne to a fat studio hack who was verbally assaulting them (or possibly physically and/or sexually assaulting them, depending on what studio they represented). Other than the setup staff and the security dudes starting their shift, the space was completely empty. Enormous and empty.

The room was set up in a particularly nonegalitarian fashion. There was a large circle on the outside that was obviously set up for the plebes. Within that was an oval of tables for the use of those who were important enough to be allowed to sit but who were not quite important enough to enter the very center of the room, where each of the *Entourage* stars had their own little enclave. Thus arranged so the stars didn't have to actually mingle with any mortal human beings. At such celebrity events, it is imperative to keep the talent as completely inaccessible as possible. Otherwise, what's the point of their celebrity?

Upon our entry, there were no celebrities or civilians present, just worker bees. I stuck out like a foreskin at a synagogue's grand opening. It was too early for us to be partygoers, and I was too debonair to be a member of the support staff. Some unconscious, innate JRLness kicked in. My mind flipped through the plausible reasons why I could possibly be in this situation and, given who I might possibly be, how I would react. A few confused glances darted my way, as various people began to notice my presence.

Obviously I was some honcho at the studio or the DVD distributor or the artists' management. I was the guy they parachuted in early to do the groundwork and make sure no one fucked up. I mean, look at me: blazer, shades, shoes that cost more than the monthly salary of that guy erecting a banner with Vince Chase's face on it. I was obviously an important dude. And that was exactly the kind of essence I tried to exude.

I slowly toured the room, my date on my arm, complimenting staff on their placement of the crab cakes, adjusting the occasional floral display, nodding expressively, and generally strutting around like I could explode into a furious spittle-flecked rage at any second if I noted even the merest suggestion of incompetence. I was the "adjuster," the "equalizer," the "commandant." Someone who was so important and so kick-ass that I didn't have a dedicated job title; I just walked in and sorted shit out.

Then I walked up to the guys on the door. This is a maneuver I would later dub "seducing security." No one ever talks to these dudes unless they have a problem or want to start a fight. But I wandered over, with my gorgeous chesty companion, and started to schmooze. Why? I needed these fuckers on my side. I didn't have an invite, I didn't have a lanyard, and I didn't have any fucking reason to be there. But if I could place myself in the minds of the security guys as someone who was definitely a legitimate member of the party, they wouldn't give me shit. I was there, so I was supposed to be there. I told them my name, shook their hands, and started my spiel.

"Don't think we've met. Just wanted to introduce myself. Harvey couldn't be here himself (I had no fucking idea who Harvey was, but it sounded like the sort of name the big guy at the top might have), but he wanted me to thank you fellows for all your great work. Maybe you could introduce me to the whole detail . . ."

I got the first security guy to introduce me to all the other security guys. I shook all their hands, looked them in the eye, and congratulated them on their excellent work. And now I had them. My hand was stamped. I made a point to remember all their first names. They couldn't throw me out now, despite my lack of credentials. I'd preempted the situation and had the chutzpah to befriend these walruses in tuxedos before they could start to consider who the fuck I was. And with that I retreated to the bar.

All the guests had been at another location, watching the season premiere. Now that was over, and the room slowly started to fill. Two things crossed my mind: First, my date was getting bored, and I needed her as an accessory to my social-criminal activity. Also, I didn't want her to leave, as I wanted to fuck her eventually. Second, and even more importantly, I, too, was getting bored. I didn't want to be orbiting the celebrities at the outer edges of this party. I needed material, and that wasn't going to happen from where I was standing. I was losing the buzz. It was time to get myself a little bump up.

At the very core of the room, where the top tier of celebrities was to be accommodated, each table had a particular high-falutin' alcoholic beverage sitting on it. There seemed to be some social status associated with this. There was Veuve Clicquot next to Perrier-Jouët and finally Cristal. The Cristal was on the table reserved for "Jeremy Piven and guests." Obviously it was the best one in the joint, reflecting Piven's stratum in this world. Sitting at the table was a guy who obviously inhabited the upper echelons of Hollywood. He looked bored. Bored in the way I look bored when I walk into a frozen-yogurt store. Like he'd seen all this shit before. My initial thought was to sidle up to this guy, shake his hand, and feed him some bullshit story. Instead, I had a far more insane idea.

I grabbed my date, strode over, sat down at Piven's table like it was my given birthright to be there, and popped the cork on the Cristal while releasing a celebratory cheer. The guy looked at me like I'd just popped his daughter's cherry. I glanced over, smiled him the sweetest beam I could muster, then slowly poured my date, and myself, a glass of extraordinarily expensive sparkling grape juice. I offered the guy some. His expression was one of complete bemusement.

"Hi," I said, extending a hand. "I'm Justin. I'm Jeremy's cousin. He wanted me to keep his table warm."

The guy cautiously told me he was Jeremy's agent from CAA. *Of course* he was. He had agent smeared all over him.

He started to question me. "So are you on his mom's or dad's side?"

Fuck, I don't know. I don't even know if he has a mom or dad. But I know who does. This fucking guy asking me the questions. It happened in a New York minute, so I didn't have the time to Google myself out of trouble.

I took a stab. "Yeah, his mom's. Hey did you meet . . . ?"

I pushed my date and her hooters toward the guy. Though in theory he was talking to me, his eyes were transfixed by that luscious cleavage. While he was distracted, I had another lunatic idea. I quickly changed a contact in my phone to read

"Cousin J." Then I got the real person whose number it was to text me. "Just message me any old shit," I told the real person. He did, and of course my phone flashed up with "Cousin J," and I made sure the agent saw it.

"Hey, Jeremy's trying to contact me. He's running late again. That asshole . . ."

Yadda, yadda, yadda. Seems crazy, I know, but it worked. This guy completely bought that I was part of the Piven clan. And that was it—I was in. I was now firmly cemented in the inner circle. And now that I was there, I made sure I stayed there. A great way to do that is to start ordering stuff. If you sit there looking meek and nervous, you'll stand out like a stiff dick at a convent. If you start yelling at servers and asking for more Cristal and blinis and smoked salmon, they're suddenly working for you. You've put yourself in charge, and obviously you're exactly where you're supposed to be. It's all about rank, and now I outranked them. This kind of bravado ensured that I wasn't going anywhere.

I'd made it onto the inside. But the important thing was to get pictures. By now the celebrities had started to drift in. The *Entourage* people were ensconced at their little tables away from the riffraff.

"Yeah, I'm going to bug Adrian," I said to the agent, and moved off. I went from table to table, feeding them the same line about being Piven's cousin and getting pictures with everyone. All the cast, all the execs, other random celebrities who happened to be around. It was great. Dynamite material. And my date was loving it. She was just dripping off me, thanks to all this celebrity contact, and she still had absolutely no idea what was happening. Before anyone could question me about my credentials or ask me salient points about Piven family history, I just edged her chest in their direction. It seemed like nothing could derail this perfect grift.

Then Jeremy Piven walked in.

I'd gotten so excited by all the high-end booze and star-spangled elbow rubbing, I'd momentarily forgotten about the lie I'd laid down to get there in the first place. Now I was looking at the angry-looking dude heading my way, who could quite easily bring this house of bullshit crashing down onto my perfectly shaped head. I saw him examining his exclusive area, which was now destroyed and liberally littered with used plates and empty bottles. I saw the words "What the fuck?" take shape on his lips. I acted fast.

I strode right up to him before anyone else could get close, slapped my arm around his shoulder, and smiled.

Then I whispered in his ear: "Hey. Great to see you. I'm Kevin Dillon's cousin."

He looked at me, openmouthed.

"I've been really enjoying your table. Kevin thought it would be really funny if I crashed it since no one else was here yet."

For a second Piven looked at me like I was a complete schmuck; then he laughed and slapped my shoulder and offered me a glass of Cristal from a bottle I'd ordered earlier on HBO's tab. This was beautiful. The agent, who could have completely blown the whole fucking thing for me, saw the two of us laughing and assumed it was cousinly love. If I may say so, it was a stroke of genius to simply switch family allegiances, and rather than be related to Piven, I just traveled one rung down the *Entourage* ladder and became Dillon's cousin instead. Then Piven bitched to me about a girl who was stuck outside and how the security wouldn't let her in.

"Leave it to me," I told him.

I walked over to my new pals, the security guards, the ones I'd ass-kissed earlier. I told them of the situation. Of course to them, I was some hotshot HBO fixer of no fixed title, so they jumped to help me. They went outside, found Piven's girl, brought her inside, and gave her the full VIP treatment. Now I wasn't just an interloper to the people in the inner circle; I was a fucking god.

We continued to party amongst the elite, but soon it was loud, it was sweaty, the music was booming, and polite conversation was impossible. No one was going to blow my cover. And the complete relief I felt at not only getting in there, but also affixing myself at the celebrity level and obtaining all the pictures I needed, was incredible.

"You know what?" I said to my date, who now thought I was the coolest fucking douche bag in this entire ZIP code, and if she wasn't going to fuck me before was certainly going to fuck me now. "This is lame. Let's split."

I wanted to be out of there at a decent celebrity time. The party would be dying soon anyway; I didn't want to be there to see it die. I waved at my cousin Kevin, I waved at my cousin Jeremy, and then I got the fuck out of there.

I eventually uploaded those pictures to Facebook and caused a mild sensation. Suddenly people were interested.

"Who is this guy with all of *Entourage*? How did he get invited to the party? He must be someone."

"I must be," I thought. "I must be someone."

And the girl with the tits? Yes.

***

I never gave a shit about celebrities when I was a kid. I only liked famous comedians.

While my family would text me if Barbara Walters was three tables over from them at Elio's on the Upper East Side, I already fully appreciated the bullshit of that situation. These people weren't special. People just acted like they were special.

They got lucky. Sure, some of them had talent, but luck was more important than any talent. Getting lucky was their fucking talent.

I loved Seinfeld and Larry David and any other purveyors of the peculiarities of the Jewish condition. So I know what you're asking: Why didn't I become a stand-up? Really? Have you ever actually met a stand-up comedian? They are the most fucked-up people on earth, who, despite their profession, seem incapable of joy. And besides, stand-up has been done. No matter how fucking hilarious I am, no matter how long I do it for or how many Adam Sandler vehicles I manage to land a costarring role in, I'm never going to be the best stand-up in the world. And if I'm not going to be the best in the world, I'm not interested.

I wanted to perform; I wanted to be known. I didn't want to break a sweat. Why try to claw your way to the front of an enormous crowd when you can be a pioneer? Sure, there might be pitfalls and snakes and hordes of angry Native Americans, but there won't be any fucking competitors on the trail you're blazing.

This is exactly what I decided to do. If I was going to be famous simply for being me, then I could use other celebrities to thoroughly lube my fame hole. It's fine; they understand. Do you think they got to where they are through their consummate skill and startling performance technique? Of course not. They rose to the top through the usual backbiting, cocksucking, and general manipulation. They know how the game is played.

Celebrities aren't people. Well, technically, they are people. Just highly agitated people. Imagine constantly being asked things.

"Hey, can you sign this?"

"Hey, can you read this?"

"Hey, can I just slip this into your mouth?"

Combine that with the complete coddling that celebrities encounter, with every whim catered to and every dreg of life taken care of, and you create someone with a pretty fucked worldview. They are all batshit crazy and faintly dangerous if cornered.

Once you hit a particular level of fame, you are basically transformed into a giant baby. You no longer have to deal with anything. *Anything.* All the mundane, distasteful, pointless facets of life are completely taken out of your hands. So if you're someone like me who enjoys fully exploiting celebrities for his own advantage, the only way to get that baby interested is to offer it something it hasn't seen before. You need to stand out. You have about four microseconds to get this putz's attention as they weigh up whether you are worthy of their indulgence, so you need to make it count.

As I found with the *Entourage* party, the familiar really helps. You claim to be a relative or the friend of a relative or lightly drop something into the conversation that validates your existence.

"Yeah, I met you at that screening. I'm [insert costar's name] brother's kid."

"Oh yeah, right."

They don't fucking know. They don't fucking care. Thirty seconds before this conversation they were probably having Vicodin blown up their ass while sipping Fresca.

"Oh yeah, I work with Kenny over at United Artists."

"I was the best boy on that last piece of shit you were in."

Just imply that you orbit their world. Make sure you don't offer anything they'll be afraid of. If you scream "I loved you in *Nutty Professor II: The Klumps*" in their face, you'll be swiftly dragged away by your hair. But they'll listen if you say, "Yeah, I was doing set continuity on *Nutty Professor II: The Klumps.* Remember that guy at the craft-services table?"

I call it my "familiarization technique." Just latch on to something they can recognize to set you apart from the herd and ensure that you're not immediately identified as a murderer or (worse) a tabloid reporter. This technique can be as blunt or as sophisticated as you like. "I'm so-and-so's cousin." That's pretty blunt. But if you want to get tricky, do like I did: I once convinced the manager of a leading actor that his client and I were fabulous pals. I changed the contact name of a friend of mine on my phone so when he texted back in real time I looked like the real deal. It might have gotten slightly out of hand.

I know that might sound completely insane, but you have to try this shit out. What's the worst that can happen? You're not going to jail for any of this. That's what I understood at that *Entourage* party. You can't get arrested for impersonating Jeremy Piven's cousin (unless you're defrauding someone for that purpose, in which case I'd pick a better target than Ari Gold). The very, very least you'll get out of it is a story. They may even admire your chutzpah as they have you thrown out. Nothing ventured, nothing gained.

Of course, all of this has to be adapted to suit the situation. If you're dealing with someone outside the sweet, fluffy world of showbiz, say a Trump or a Clinton, there's no point buttering them up or dropping shit about being someone's kinfolk. Unlike actors, those people are smart. You need to challenge them. Not that anyone would, but don't bother telling the Donald that you loved *The Art of the Deal* or that his hair is "really neat." That will sail right over his well-coiffured head. It's better to critique his work and then tell him why. Or say, "I really enjoyed that speech you made, and here's where you got everything wrong." They adore that shit.

So what's the point of all this celebrity sucking up? Celebrities are currency. You exchange their notoriety for your own purposes. Whether it's getting a picture taken with them, using their name to get you into the papers, or acting as if they are your best friend in the whole fucking world, you manipulate their elevated status to promote your own. No one gives a fuck who you are. But if you are next to a Kardashian, then that's a story. If you are next to a Kardashian who has their hands around your throat, that's an even better story. (And by the way, if OJ Simpson had just taken a Xanax on that fateful night, there wouldn't even be any Kardashians. Surely a more notable reason to jail him.)

For instance, I got a lot of air mileage from a JewJetting incident with Ashley Olsen, the lesser of the Olsen twins. She had the misfortune of sitting next to me in first class (obviously) on a flight between Los Angeles and New York City. For many, that would be the extent of the story: "I sat next to an Olsen twin! On one occasion! She even spoke to me! Sort of!" But I knew I could wring a huge amount of exposure out of this good fortune.

She already seemed fairly damaged when she sat down, exuding the privileged contrariness of celebrity. Someone helped her frail frame onto the plane, guided her to her seat, and dealt with her luggage. She proceeded to crawl under a $2,000 cashmere Hermès throw and tried to obliterate any thoughts about who she was. Basically she drank, lay down, and fell asleep. But with a few surreptitious photographs, I was able to convince *Star* magazine that I spent a glorious few hours in the air "sleeping with an Olsen twin" and reporting on her "wacky behavior." Was Ashley that wacky? Who gives a shit? When the bullshit is better than the story, print the bullshit.

People loved the idea that I pretended not to know who she was and called her Amy throughout the flight, only revealing everything to her at the baggage claim. It extended my legend. The story was picked up in various papers and blogs, and my pretentious *punim* was sitting there right next to Ashley's. It was glitz by association, and it kept the JRL choo choo rolling, pushing me a few more column inches up the hill. And was Ashley "harmed"? Who cares, she's richer than foie gras blintzes.

You may need to exaggerate, elaborate, cajole, and outright fib, but the important thing is to own the narrative, good or bad. Most people are naturally inclined to want a positive outcome during an encounter with a celebrity. But sometimes that's just not the most profitable direction. Take my altercation with Star Jones. I had my picture taken next to her, which I could have just posted and then moved on with my life. Hardly anyone would have noticed, and an equal amount of people would have cared. But print a picture of her that includes a thought bubble displaying an image of some Devil Dogs? That is going to get some mileage. I made sure the world knew of her outrage, which led to me being banned from a number of high-profile locations due to Star's wrath. All parties concerned were wounded and appalled, but I managed to spin that story out far beyond its expiration date.

You also have to establish the right target. There's no point in me propagating a feud with someone like Sandra Bullock. People actually like Sandra Bullock. Sure, if I could get a picture with her, that would be great. But if I tried to pull some Ashley/Star bullshit with her, it wouldn't fly. She's too beloved. Same with Paul Rudd. I attempted to get something going with that asshole but soon discovered no one really cared. People were aware of his existence but hadn't really formulated an opinion about him. Your targets have to be either loved or hated for them to be significant—hated being better than loved. Prove that someone who is known for being a dickhead is being a dickhead, and that will run and run.

What matters is eliciting a reaction. As the upcoming case studies will illustrate, it's win-win once the wheels are set in motion. If a celebrity ignores you (which is always the most sensible response), then great! You own the story and can mold it into any shape you wish. If you do provoke them into action (usually through "their people"), even better! You respond, they respond, you say something else inflammatory, and they get outraged; it's the gift that just keeps giving.

The best approach when dealing with celebrities is to not have any loyalties, any heroes, or any preconceived notions. I wanted to be notable, but on my own terms. So I became a celebrity on my own terms. Through sheer force of will. I was a celebrity. That was it. I told people I was one, I certainly acted like one, and I lived like one. I was one. Am I more worthless than Rick from *Pawn Stars*? That guy gets to enjoy celebrity status by working in a store. I'm supposed to act like I'm lower down the ladder than someone like him? Fuck that shit. Being a celebrity isn't hard; you just have to convince yourself you are one. Surprisingly, there's no entrance exam to get in and no one to kick you out. All you need in order to own it is major chutzpah and the ability to think on your feet. And now I'm actually treated like a celebrity. Where once I was riding on the immense coattails of Star Jones, people now write about JRL. Just JRL. I'm the focus of the story. As we will discuss later, in certain parts of the world I'm fucking bigger than a Baldwin brother. Just for being me. Hey, I know that shit is crazy, but what can I do?

But before all that, here are some more prime examples of celebrity interaction and the rewards it can reap . . .

Case Study: Brad Pitt

Always follow the valets. If they are dressed fancy and looking nervous, you know some shit is going down. Plus they are usually fairly disgruntled and will happily give up information if it provides an outlet to bitch about their appalling lives. And the valets surrounding the Mondrian were supersquirrelly.

I was in Los Angeles and staying at that swanky location (comped, natch). Even in this rarified atmosphere, I could tell something big was happening. Then I found out what was happening. Brad Pitt was happening. The Mondrian Hotel was to be the location of the premiere party for *Inglourious Basterds*. All the stars would be there. Including Brad Pitt. Actual premieres are boring as shit, but premiere parties are a prime location for celebrity action.

Now, I have no preconceived notions about Brad. From what I can gather, he's a perfectly reasonable, decent guy who just happens to be the most famous male face on the planet. Which translates as complete inaccessibility. You can never get anywhere near him. That makes him a challenge. I wanted Brad Pitt. A picture of Mr. Jolie and me would be like all my Hanukkahs come at once.

My techniques and strategies had developed significantly since the formative days of the *Entourage* party, but this was still going to be difficult, even for an arch manipulator like me. I had the advantage of being a guest in the hotel, so I could legitimately be in the area, but I knew I would not be able to get within fifty feet of that party before a large black man wrestled me to the ground and stood on my neck.

I'd been to events at the Mondrian before—I knew the layout. Obviously I couldn't approach from the front. There was no way I could charm my way in there. (I have unlimited amounts of charm, but this was the Weinstein Company's show and Brad Pitt was on the menu. I'd be midway through my charming spiel when I'd feel the warm red dot of a sniper's sight on my forehead.) I had no big-busted accomplice to grease the wheels. I knew I'd have to bum-rush my way in and play it by ear.

I decided to case the joint. I walked up an innocuous set of concrete stairs at the back of the building until I knew I was within the vicinity of the event. There was a plain, unsuspecting door in front of me. I had no idea what was behind it. It could have been the kitchens, the hotel detective's office, or I could have hit the jackpot. My heart was in my mouth, and my matzo balls ached. They do that when I'm anxious.

I hit the door hard and walked through with a flourish. I came face to face with three of the biggest, baddest, blackest bouncers I had ever seen. These guys were huge. They could have easily been linebackers, if I had any idea what that term meant. I had two choices: go back the way I came, or forward into death. Obviously I chose death.

I approached the hugest of these dudes, prison-rules-style, and smacked that motherfucker as hard as I could on the shoulder. He barely flinched. I followed this up with, "We got people arriving in forty-five. Look alive, fellas." There was a potentially cataclysmic pause as they stared at me as if I'd just casually slipped my predilection for cross burning into the conversation. They looked at each other, and then they looked at me. Then one of them said, "Yes, boss," and stood aside.

Even for me this was ballsy. I'd just managed to bamboozle the bouncers by instructing them to keep an eye out for people exactly like me. Seducing security—it works every time. I strode right through them and into the party.

Again I was sensationally early. A few industry types eyed me with suspicion. I walked right up to them and introduced myself. That's always the way to allay suspicion—just take the initiative. An intruder would try to hide. To make it clear that you are exactly where you're supposed to be, just act like that's exactly where you are supposed to be. It's like dogs. Appear nervous and they are going to bite you on the taint. I spun a yarn to the few people there, telling them I was from the New York ICM office, my flight got screwed up, I was late for the screening and early to the party. A story they could all understand. And I used my real name. I always use my own name. It's so easy to forget a fake one. They bought it. Why wouldn't they? I was just like them. I was a cocky douche bag.

The party filled, and I took a few pictures and bullshitted with John Krasinski, but I couldn't land the white whale. Brad was behind protection, who were themselves protected by protection. All I got from the evening was a dumb World War II dog-tag thing that everyone at the party received as a gift. You get used to rejection and failure in this game.

So my trip was over and I headed home. I waited in the United Airlines first-class lounge (of course) at LAX, and who should stride in but Mr. Brad Pitt himself. Still protected, but nothing like the levels of the evening before. Here was my chance to strike. I waited until he was standing next to something attainable (the juice bar, the bagel counter, that kind of shit) and walked right up. With a star of the magnitude of Brad, who has actual, neck-snapping bodyguards constantly around him, you have much less time to make an impression. Even in the first-class lounge.

"Brad, hi, Justin, we met last night. Sarah Silverman introduced us."

I'd seen Brad, from a distance, sitting next to Sarah Silverman the previous evening. I could tell that his brain was rifling through all the prospective warning signs as his guards instinctively reached inside their jackets. (For what I have no idea. We were in an airport—I can't imagine they were packing heat).

"Oh yeah, right," he said, obviously unsure.

Then I remembered the dumb dog tag they'd given us from the party. It was still in my blazer's pocket. I whipped it out.

"This fucking thing set off the alarm coming through security. Did you get one of these?"

I dangled it in front of him.

"Yeah, yeah."

He recognized the dumb thing and knew I was legit. His heavies backed off. He smiled an actual smile rather than the smile he reserves for people who decide to hassle him. We chitchatted about the biz, and then I said, "Can I get a picture to send to Sarah?"

He obliged. I got my picture. It took some work, and some luck, but I got my picture. You take your chances; you think on your feet. You exploit every opportunity. You use the familiar. I had props; that helped.

That picture has been used everywhere. *Everywhere.*

Case Study: Kris Humphries

I hate jocks. I couldn't give a shit about sports. The only reason I recognized Kris Humphries at the Bunker (a typically hideous Manhattan club usually filled with people like me) was because he had been banging a Kardashian. I forget which one. Tito?

They had been married. It was a disaster. The nuptials were annulled, and there was a lot of speculation about Kris and his intentions. What the fuck had happened? What would happen next? I saw my opportunity. Here are all the assets I had: there was Kris and his entourage, there was me and my camera, and there was a cute willowy blond waitress. I just put Jew and Jew together and came up with four.

I approached Kris—super nice and humble—had my picture taken with him, and all was peachy. But then, as the legend goes, I saw him hitting on the waitress and completely striking out. I went back up to him and gave him shit about being able to get the waitress's digits and succeeding where he had failed. And maybe that's exactly what I did. I saw him flounder, I strode up to the girl in question, and I made her laugh and got her number (which I instantly deleted).

And then somehow this whole sorry tale got leaked to the press and telegraphed around the world. "Kris Is over Kim." "Kris Is on the Prowl Again." "Kris Shoots and Comes Up Short." "Kris Is Blocked at the Hoop by JRL." (I honestly think the abundance of sports and basketball analogies helped keep this story in the press.) No one actually checked the story. Who is going to check? If they asked me, I'd say, "Sure, that's how it went down." Think they are going to look for the waitress? "We don't know what you're talking about," the Bunker's management would trot out, fueling the flames with some vague bullshit.

And Mr. Humphries? In a fabulous stroke of good fortune, his people chose to react. After some light goading (by me) on Twitter, they released a furious press statement denying the whole thing, claiming it never happened and how Kris was a wonderful human being and probably about to get the Nobel Prize for Non-Douchery. Excellent. Now I could retaliate and deny the denial: "Kris is just upset that I was able to make a three-second violation all over that waitress." (Look, it's just too good an analogy to pass up.) It got me a couple more days in the paper.

So what was the truth? Did Kris strike out with that hottie, and did I swoop in and seduce her right under his nose? Or did I just get my picture taken with Kris Humphries and then build a plausible story around it, a story I knew the press wouldn't be able to resist? As Confucius so sagely said, "Who gives a shit?"

CHAPTER 5

JEWJETTING: I GIVE A FLYING FUCK

Have you ever taken fucking Ambien?

This shit will kick your ass. I had absolutely no idea. I assumed it was as twee and lame as its name suggests, sounding, as it does, like a sexually ambiguous Disney fairy princess. But no, it's a total monster. Which the common user doesn't usually discover until they've taken a batch, at altitude, with alcohol.

Not that I need any excuses for appalling aviation behavior. There's not too much shit I haven't done at thirty-eight thousand feet, and as my career has progressed I've just become more flagrant and unacceptable. These days I'm fucking, sucking, and then Facebooking in some first-class suite on practically a daily basis. When this particular misdemeanor I'm about to recount took place, I hadn't quite reached these heady heights yet. Though this little adventure certainly sent me on my way.

So I was flying to Frankfurt, I think. There were certainly a lot of Germans all around me. My kikey sense was tingling. And I was definitely in 1A. I mean, of course I was, but I am a storyteller and I'm trying to set the scene. Nothing untoward occurred initially. I got in, buttered up the staff, had a couple of Johnnie Walkers and hobnobbed with the locals. I unfurled my bed and changed into my jammies. I'd scored some Ambien from somewhere and so popped a couple with my scotch and settled back for a nap.

But I didn't really fall asleep. Or maybe I did for a couple of minutes, but then I entered some kind of bizarre, euphoric, sleepwalking state over Nova Scotia where I had a sudden driving desire to fuck shit up. Feeling a little cotton mouthed, I decided my thirst needed to be quenched and that champagne was the only way to go. I looked around but couldn't see any crew anywhere. So I set off in search of provisions.

Most of my privileged counterparts were snoring lightly as I headed to the galley and started to root around. I came across a few bottles that looked pretty tasty, frostily sitting there like some bubbling, icy slut. I decided to toast my good fortune and crack it open immediately. A few Germans stirred and snorted (in German) as the cork popped, but nobody tried to tackle me.

As I tipsily chugged my brut, I looked beyond my slumbering companions at the curtain in the distance.

"Just think," I pondered to myself. Or possibly said out loud, due to my fucked-up-ness. "Here I am, sipping this delicious champagne, while just a few feet away, divided by that sliver of fabric, are poor unfortunates being force-fed swill while cramped painfully in understuffed seats."

Or I think that's what I thought. Quite possibly it was closer to "Flarh, glarh, beent tad, quango" in my condition. As I've mentioned, I was pretty wasted.

This hideous economic disparity brought out my inner Bono, and I suddenly decided that I had to help the poor orphans trapped in steerage. I took the bottle and sashayed up the aisle, and dramatically emerged through the dividing curtain like I was in a high school production of *Cabaret*. Certainly, there were a few baffled Teutonic expressions as they took in this swaying, grinning, pajama-clad maniac holding champagne.

"Who wants a drink?" I asked, and then started to dispense the bottle to the grateful beneficiaries like some demented, soon-to-be-defrocked priest. Thankful Germans offered me a nervous "*Danke*" as I liberally sprayed expensive beverage in their direction.

By now, the lazy, lazy cabin crew, who had been loitering in the rear of the fuselage, realized something was going on. Something unusual. A carefully coiffured head appeared near the rear bathrooms and then quickly vanished. Then two heads reappeared and surveyed the scene. I could see the wheels spinning in their minds as they tried to conjure up the right reaction to this extraordinary situation. I think they soon realized that subtlety may be lost on a person such as myself and brute force was probably the best way to go. The woman with the most severe hairstyle was selected to approach me.

"Sir," she began as I lightly moistened another German wrist with bubbly. "What are you doing?"

Given the circumstances, I felt this was a pretty fair question.

"The people," I slurred. "These people. They have no champagne. I must give them champagne."

I tried to scoot around her to continue my campaign. But she stood firm.

"No, sir," she tried. "You cannot do this. You must return to your seat immediately."

"But I must do this," I added, then stated grandly, "You see, I am the Jewish Robin Hood."

In my Ambien-addled mind, I heard a faint cheer rise from the cheap seats as I made my pronouncement. They were my serfs; I was their savior. In reality, I imagine most of them were quite scared. The stewardess looked appalled, as if I had taken the name of Robin Hood in vain.

"You are contravening a number of airline-security protocols."

Her colleague behind her got into the tackle position: knees bent, arms outstretched to bear-hug me into submission if necessary.

"If you do not comply immediately, you will be restrained. Restrained."

She repeated the word to make it completely clear that this was the worst possible thing that could happen in the air.

"Madam . . . ," I began.

"I am the purser," she corrected.

"Look. Yes. You are the purser. And I'm Robin Hood!" I semi-bellowed.

The cuff of my in-flight PJs was lightly gripped, and someone authoritatively tried to shift my momentum back toward the curtain.

"Hey, hey, hey," I said. "I'm from first."

This evocation of the class system seemed to stir something inside them. My cuff was dropped, and they now hovered around me, caught in some weird limbo. They knew they had to defuse this situation, but, as a premium-class passenger, I'd paid for the privilege of pretty much doing whatever the fuck I liked. Finger banging very much included.

"I'm getting the captain," the purser mouthed.

There was an audible gasp from the passengers around me.

"Yeah!" I said. "Let's get this party started!"

Before I could get the party started, the captain appeared. He seemed to flit between mild amusement and slight disdain.

"Sir," he stated. "I am the captain."

(I imagine all captains start every sentence with "I am the captain," regardless of the situation—buying bagels, renting a car, getting a cheap blow job in a downtown Bangkok massage parlor.)

"I was informed of your behavior, and you must return to your seat immediately."

"Can't I come with you?" I mock pleaded. "You can take me back to the cockpit. I'd like it up there. I'd just sit quietly."

"Passengers are never allowed to enter the cockpit," the purser said, close to disgusted tears.

"It's OK," the captain said, taking over. "Listen, fella, you're angling for a written warning, or to be met at the gate if you keep this up."

"I'd love a written warning!" I said, delighted. "I've never had one of those before!"

"Great," he said. "So, if we give you a written warning, you'll go back to your seat and behave?"

"Sure." Somehow his warped logic and my warped brain were in total alignment. I'd also started to get really, really sleepy. I'd been chugging the champagne backwash and started to feel quite nicely sedated.

A steward ahead of me took my hand while the purser held the back of my PJs like she was walking me down the aisle. Which she was, I guess. They dropped me in my seat and prepared to leave, trying to put the whole thing behind them.

"Wait!" I demanded. "Where's my written warning?"

"Fine!"

The purser vanished, then returned with a hastily scribbled form that relayed my appalling behavior to the world.

"Any more outbursts," she told me, "and you will be met at the gate by authorities and taken into custody."

I started to think about whether I should double down and try for that. But while I was weighing this up in my mind, I drifted off into a deep, blissful sleep. I woke up as we were landing—refreshed, revived, and utterly despised by the entire onboard team.

***

As you may remember, if you are paying the adequate attention that I demand and deserve, my childhood dream was to become a pilot. Thank fuck I never realized that dream. Thank fuck for me and for the people living under my imagined flight path. Being a pilot is a one-mistake career. I tend to attract mistakes. I probably would have died on day one. In the flight simulator.

Or the best I could have hoped for would be to have been fired on day one, immediately after my first landing. I mean, can you imagine a sarcastic pilot? A snarky captain? That's my only setting! There's no way I could sit there with an intercom at my disposal and not try out some material. I would surely be led from the cockpit to a soundtrack of screams, tears, and baffled abuse.

Knowing I could never be the best pilot in the world, I decided to become the best passenger in the world. And this revelation reached me due to the deadly combination of pity and pussy. And, as inevitably occurs, some pity pussy. And pussy followed by pity. All combinations were represented. Let's deal with the pity first.

Earlier we learned of my miraculous community service after a pretty virulent Super Bowl riot that I accidentally initiated. Through a variety of devious means, I'd managed to transfer this community service to some hippy-soaked project in rural Brazil. I was ecstatic that I'd turned my incarceration into vacation, but I wasn't really looking forward to that eleven-hour flight in coach.

I'd not yet developed the techniques and maneuvers to guarantee an upgrade. I just knew I didn't want to be sitting next to a fat chick with a mustache and an accent for half a day. So I was flying blind when I approached the desk and tried it on with the counter staff.

"Yeah, I think I'm due for an upgrade," I tried.

The clicking of computer keys. "Uh . . . nope. I don't think so, sir."

"I applied a certificate. Really? Can you check again?"

More clicking. "No, I can't see anything."

"Let me talk to your duty manager."

After a whispered telephone conversation, a man who was born to play a duty manager appeared. I took him aside.

"Listen, I really think there has been a mistake with my seat allocation, and I actually should be in 1A? Could you see if that's possible?"

I'd been given a wad of cash by my family for the trip. Just in case I got kidnapped or contracted some exotic venereal disease. I knew I wouldn't need that amount of money. I was venturing into the third world, after all. So I handed this guy my ticket with $500 slipped inside.

He was silent for a while. Then he looked at me with pure disgust, tinged with disappointment. Like I'd just spit on his daughter's pussy. He was truly appalled.

"At the very least, the *very least*, I'd lose my job," he lamented. "Quite possibly we'd both be going to jail. What are you thinking? I would never degrade the good name of this airline or the responsibility bestowed upon me . . ."

On and on he went. Eventually he ran out of steam, and I talked to him mano a mano.

"Calm down. I'm not the first guy to try and bribe his way into an upgrade. You don't need to get medieval. I tried and fucked up; you can save the sermon."

I think he grasped that he may have gone overboard to a certain degree, and eventually he started talking to me like a human being and gave me his card. Which I considered a valuable prop.

With that utter failure behind me, I checked in and joined the cattle by the gate. But I still didn't want to sit in fucking coach. So I pieced together a pretty half-assed plan. Once on board, I stowed my stuff above a seat in business class (I'd felt it would be pushing it to try for first), then headed into the bathroom. I stayed in there for a good twenty minutes, releasing the occasional sound of gastric exertion whenever anyone checked on me. After the plane doors had been closed and locked, I appeared and took an empty seat in business.

Predeparture drinks were served, smiles were offered, and the usual procedures began. Then a few worried expressions appeared. A hushed conversation amongst the cabin crew was followed by a prolonged period of head counting. Staff walked up and down the plane, trying to calculate the bodies in seats, with puzzled looks on their faces. Eventually an announcement was made.

"Sorry about this slight delay, folks. Just have a slight problem with the passenger manifest. We'll get this sorted out, and we'll be on our way in fifteen or twenty minutes."

Then the crew began to go from seat to seat, checking everyone's ticket. I'd never seen anything like that before. Eventually they realized that I was the problem.

"Sir, we think you are in the wrong seat?"

"No," I said casually. "I'm in the right seat. And can I get another glass of champagne since we're delayed?"

"But if you look at your ticket you've been assigned—"

"I was promised an upgrade by your duty manager; perhaps he just forgot to manifest it. If you contact him, he'll sort everything out. Here's his card. What are the appetizers on this flight?"

I handed over his card and hoped he'd finished his shift so they'd be unable to reach him and they'd give me the benefit of the doubt. Meanwhile we heard from the captain . . .

"Folks, sorry about this extended delay. I'm afraid we've now missed our takeoff window. We are working with air traffic control to find us a new slot, and then we'll be on our way, hopefully in just a few minutes."

Then the guys upstairs did get back in touch. Or at least that one guy whose name I had tried to exploit. I didn't hear what he'd said, but I assume it was along the lines of "What the fuck! That little prick tried to bribe me, and now he's using my name to get some bullshit upgrade? Do we have time to off-load him? Does he have baggage in the hold? Let me call operations and see what they want to do."

I've encountered many cabin crew with pissy expressions on their faces in my time, but nothing like this. These guys wanted to fuck me fervently with a blunt instrument. What was worse, after they'd informed me that we wouldn't be going anywhere until I got into my assigned seat, I was forced to undergo a walk of shame back to coach. My fellow passengers, realizing I was the source of the delay, were less than sympathetic to my cause. That was a pretty tense flight.

I had been fucking humiliated. I mean, I appreciated the balls that I'd displayed by trying this shit in the first place, and, with a favorable wind, on another day I might have pulled it off. But I knew that if I wanted to stay out of coach forever, I would have to up my game. Devise some slightly more sophisticated techniques than simply hiding in the bathroom and praying for a miracle. I needed to put in some serious flying hours to work out the kinks. And that's when the pussy offered me the opportunity.

Her name was Heather. She was an American-Parisian socialite, and a fucking ass load of trouble. I met her on the Champs-Élysées. She didn't walk into a room; she floated in. Her charm and allure were next level. All I can remember is seeing this vision of Gallic loveliness and knowing I had to get to know her. We couldn't venture into certain parts of the city, we couldn't be too flagrant about our relationship, and we couldn't go to her place. She was really devious and had a different excuse for the shadiness every time. She obviously had all sorts of rackets going on. Drooling dudes in every arrondissement. But man, she was worth it. I totally fell for her and had to see her at every opportunity. But how? She lived in Paris, and I was trapped in Hartford, Connecticut.

It was then I started to study. Not at school (obviously), but I tried to figure out the secrets of air travel. I looked into air miles and the attached offers and schemes. You see, most people fly a couple of times a year at most. They steadily accrue their miles (if they bother at all) and never consider the angles, letting them expire most times before taking full advantage. Those people who fly all the time (for work) tend to do it on someone else's dime. Their company is picking up the tab, so they don't give a shit about saving money or grabbing mileage. So most of these offers are ignored or overlooked. But to an operator like me, they are just waiting to be exploited.

So I started figuring out every single fucking thing about aviation. The ridiculous lexicon, the best airlines, the places to sit, the ones to avoid. And, I admit it, I became an absolute nerd about it. I worked out things like taking four or so internal flights that cost nothing, which can accrue you enough miles to get you across the Atlantic. I could pick up a few credit cards, make a few bullshit purchases, and grab even more miles. Soon I was flying over to France every other weekend for a spell of light continental boning followed by a hot croissant.

Eventually I realized I'd fallen out of love with Heather and into love with the high life. So I stopped shtupping her and started to fly just for the hell of it. And not just fly, but fly in style. I'd read about that classy, swinging, Pan Am style of aviation. All miniskirted stewardesses waddling down the aisle and handing you cocktails as you sucked on a Lucky Strike. I decided to start a one-man campaign to bring those days back. Or else live in a delusion where I believed those days still existed. Which, you must admit, is a lovely place to be.

And there was another reason it attracted me to such a degree. Flying is unique. As well as being utterly magical, disrupting all notions of human achievability and crapping all over understandable physics, it's also the only institution where any sort of class system is still vigorously enforced. You see, the world used to be all about class. There were the "betters" and the "worse offs." Everyone knew their place, which provided a certain amount of comfort. You didn't have to try, because there was no point. You just lived in your hut, got used to the smell of sewage, and assumed that at least a few of your children wouldn't make it to adulthood. Everything was peachy.

Then "democracy" raised its unwashed head. Suddenly everyone felt that they deserved to be just as good as everyone else. And everything went to shit. Expectations were raised, idiots lined up to be abused on talent shows, and every teenage girl had a blog chronicling her self-harm.

But none of that exists in the skies. The caste system is still firmly in place, and I couldn't be happier about it. And despite desperate attempts to tone down the language and apply a few less offensive pseudonyms to the system, it's still known as "first class" and "second class." You can make reference to "economy" or "world traveler" or "main cabin," but we all know what these euphemisms mean. Steerage. A cramped, painful seat next to a sweaty man with a flatulence problem and behind an old lady who treats her recliner like a goddamned rocking chair. Some have even discussed planning to make you pay to use the bathroom. *To use the bathroom.* You're already paying to possess possessions, hydrate, and look out a window. It's one thing to pay a little less and endure a less comfortable experience. But this is the stripping of basic human rights. What the fuck happened to flying?

Meanwhile, the divide between the shit you face in coach and glorious luxuries of first class increases exponentially. Now you get suites up there. Rooms with walls. You can happily saunter from one part of your personal cabin to the other. You can break-dance. You can limbo. And you can fuck.

Which, let's face it, is what all this is about. The creation and eternal improvement of the upper-class section of the airplane were designed solely so rich people can fuck in peace. Because that's what rich people do. They fuck. All the time. Mostly people over. And they assume they can fuck any place they want. And they can. Because they are rich.

So are you still asking yourself, "Why would JRL want to dedicate his life to the acquisition of this?" Yeah, why would I want to be surrounded by luxury and have hot- and cold-running pussy, plus a button I could push for champagne or caviar or a fresh duvet to be brought directly to me? Flying first class is a fairy tale. For the length of the flight, you are royalty. Pampered, polished, and pandered to by a dedicated staff and surrounded by like-minded sociopaths. To live this life on the ground takes years of dedicated hard work or else the good fucking fortune of being born into it. It's something that hardly any of us can hope for. But getting into first class and staying there is *easy*. You just have to master the system; take the rules and fuck them a little.

So not only did I fuck the rules. I also gave it a name: JewJetting.

What the Fuck Is JewJetting?

First, you need to make a little alteration of consciousness.

You need to embrace the idea of traveling and getting nowhere. Jettisoning the destination. Ditching the departure board. Not even considering where you are headed until you see the Eiffel Tower or the Sydney Opera House under the wing. And even then you can barely give a shit. Because those are the fundamentals of JewJetting.

And that's it. It's all done for the joy of doing it. Frankly, if you can't quite grasp that, then there's a wonderful seat waiting for you way down at the end of the fuselage. Right next to the bathroom and in the perfect target zone for the sharp elbows of a dusty stewardess who seems to be colliding with you for fun or punishment. You can always comfort yourself with the thought that we all die with urine in our pants if this plane goes down, no matter where you are sitting. Though, to be honest, it doesn't cross my mind much as I recline to 180 degrees and sip my luxury cocktail.

And there was a wonderful side effect to all this extravagance. People were interested in it. And consequently, they were interested in me. Once my exploits, like the Robin Hood incident, started to get written up in blogs and make the news, people started asking themselves, "Who is this asshole and how did he get into first class?" I started to chronicle my JewJetting exploits, which caused further consternation and even more fascination with my douchery. Then I figured out that I didn't even have to do that much. There was no need to repeat lunacy and get further written warnings. All I had to do was take a picture. If I documented something salacious or ludicrous or unbelievably fucking decadent, my stock rose exponentially. It was fantastic. I was doing what I loved and, as a consequence, consolidating my brand. It was all gravy.

A far more sensible question, which gets fired at me constantly, is how the fuck I manage to do all this. As an answer, let me tell you a little story.

On one occasion, I found myself in first class (of course) sitting next to a man I recognized from an in-flight magazine. He would mean very little to you, but to me this was a figure of inspiration and also my archenemy. He was my tormentor and my victim. He was Doug Parker, the CEO of US Airways. The fucking CEO of the airline that I fly on the most, right here next to me—a captive audience. The odds of being seated next to this man are staggering.

(That is another wonderful aspect of air travel. There is no escape. Whoever is in the section with you stays in the section with you, giving you the opportunity to schmooze, pitch, photograph, or harass to your heart's content.)

Anyway, I'm sitting there with Doug Parker. (I should mention we were not traveling on his particular carrier. He's smart enough not to always fly on company metal and get suckered into serving Sprite Zero or wishing people happy birthday and that kind of shit). I waited until we are airborne, and then I turned to him.

"Hi," I said to him. "I'm Justin Ross Lee, and I have been legally fleecing your company for years. I'm currently Silver on your airline. Change my status to Chairman's Preferred, and I'll tell you everything."

He looked at me like I was crazy. But here we were in first class. So if I was crazy, I was crazy and had access to money. Or I did have some secrets to share.

"Really?" he said with worry.

I told him all about one of the many schemes that I invented and regularly exploited with glee. Being a Preferred member of US Airways Dividend Miles (when the airline and program existed) means you can get an upgrade to first class if there are seats available and if those higher up in the cardholding food chain don't bag those seats first. Except they always bag those seats first. At the time a twenty-five-thousand-mile-per-year schlub like me would never snatch a seat by legitimate means. So how can I ensure that I get my sweet little ass into 1A?

Weeks before a flight, I go online and buy refundable tickets for every single seat in first. Remember, you need *refundable* tickets, or else you've just made an incredibly expensive blooper. I've now completely sold out first class. And not only sold it out, but also assigned each seat to someone with a comical name. Just for funsies. So you can have John Hinkley next to Jodie Foster. Kim Kardashian next to Albert Einstein. Rambo next to Rocky. Any old shit. Then, a few days before the flight, I cancel all these seats. I get the money back on my credit cards. Then I'd immediately call the airline . . .

"Hey, I am ticketed on the two-thirty flight to Miami, and I noticed that first class is completely empty. I'm not sure what happened to your system's sweep at my upgrade window, but I was hoping, as a loyal Silver, you can manually process my upgrade."

"Golly!" they say (or similar). "That's weird. No one is in first. Sure, we can do that for you."

So I get a seat in first. It takes a little effort and conjuring up a bunch of dumb names, but there you go. First class every time. Sometimes I'd book a refundable ticket and not go any-where. Just head to the lounge, conduct my business, stock up on free booze, and then have my ticket refunded. All for the price of an Uber.

"But that's just wrong," Old Doug tells me. "You're just a swindler."

"But I'm not," I joyfully tell him. "It's a loophole. Check out your own contract of carriage. Nothing legally dubious is tak-ing place. It's as kosher as I am. And I'm pretty fucking kosher." (I had bacon that very morning).

And he had to agree with me. He was impressed with my candor, and we actually hit it off. He gave me his card and eventually had his personal assistant bump me up to the top tier, Chairman's Preferred, so I didn't have to pull that kind of shit anymore (on that particular airline).

They've changed the rules now, but this is just one of a myriad of ways I fuck these companies. It's a constant battle with them. They work out there's something going on, they change their rules, and I find another hole.

For instance, there are always ridiculous offers and deals relating to air miles. Back when I was a rookie JewJetter, one airline had an online-shopping-mall-portal promotion part-nering with the Sharper Image for the holidays. Pretty simple stuff: earn twenty or twenty-five miles per dollar spent online. So I would order online for in-store pickup and saunter down to the Sharper Image to fetch one of those pointless, ridiculous $3,000 massage chairs designed for desperate middle-manage-ment executives to blow their bonuses. I'd walk in, have the chair placed in the back of a Grand Cherokee, drive straight over to another Sharper Image, return the dumb chair, and get the refund put on another card (telling them the original form of payment was lost or stolen). I'd get the miles for the purchase and the money for the refund. Positive net.

I'd do this several times a week, until the guys at the Sharper Image thought I was some kind of weird, chair-sniffing deviant. But by this method I had generated hundreds of thousands of miles, more than enough to circumnavigate the globe a few times on my back. Yeah, it was a pain in the ass to hump chairs all over the place and interact with that certain level of desperation you only find in stores like the Sharper Image—but who cares when you can roll those miles over into a first-class seat to Tokyo?

I'd spend all of my time scouring the press for these types of deals: taking out credit cards with air miles attached (I think I was up to about $250,000 in credit at my zenith), looking for promotional deals with airline hookups, planning internal flights with tons of stopovers that just cost a couple hundred bucks but clocked up massive amounts of extra points.

It's an addiction. You get obsessed with accumulating these things and swapping tips with fellow junkies online who also do this shit. It can be hard work, and you need a decent grasp of organization and spreadsheets, but it's worth it. A nice lounge to sit in. No bullshit with security. No waiting at the gate. Gourmet food and nonstop pampering. And then there's the slightly more dubious perks.

I love Johnnie Walker Blue Label. But that shit is expensive. Sitting in first, you obviously get it for bubkes. I was taking a flight to Hong Kong, I think. I asked for some Johnnie Walker Blue. They brought over a one-and-a-half-liter bottle of the stuff. Massive and with a cherry that had yet to be popped.

"I don't want to keep bothering you; just leave the bottle if you want," I told my server with nonchalance.

They left this massive amount of premium booze, knowing I couldn't do that much damage to it. But they were wrong. Horribly, horribly wrong. I'd also been ordering Perrier throughout the flight. Why? Perrier bottles are colored in such a way that they disguise anything. Including Johnnie Walker Blue Label. I funneled the juice into the bottles—using the glossy, pointless in-flight magazine—and stowed it in my carry-on. At the end of the flight, a disturbed crew member came and collected this enormous, empty liquor bottle. Obviously, if I'd drunk all that I should be dead at the very least. But I soberly gave him my warmest regards and alighted as smugly as possible.

Do you think that's stealing? But how can it be? It's free! If I'd sat patiently in my seat and downed this entire bottle of whisky, it would have been thoroughly unpleasant but totally legitimate in the eyes of the moral world. I just applied the doggie-bag rule and got a lot of lovely booze to enjoy at my leisure. It's a perk! You got any tiny bottles of hotel "body lotion" in your bathroom? Of course you do! Everyone does and everyone is a hypocrite.

Even if you're trapped in coach there are tricks you can pull to make your trip less harrowing. One thing I always used to travel with? A small baggie of ground-up peanuts. If you get seated between a vomiting baby and an obese midwesterner eating a Subway sandwich, just whip out your nuts. Sprinkle a few crumbs on your seat and your tray table, and then alert the crew. Inform them that you have a deadly nut allergy and your lovely seat is practically *caked* with detritus. They have to reseat you. They *have* to. If you start swelling up midair because the staff don't like the look of you and an emergency landing is required, that costs the airline a dickful of money. It makes more sense for them to find you a new spot to inhabit, maybe even an upgrade if they've oversold the fucking thing.

And if you've been a victim of lost luggage on a number of occasions, a great way to never have your bag mislaid is to travel with a firearm. I'm being completely serious. Take a starter pistol, stick it in the luggage you're checking in, and then make sure you tell them at the counter. You're doing nothing wrong. You need a starter pistol for your job as an international pussy inspector. And you've been completely honest and up-front with them. But, knowing they have a firearm in the hold, that bag will be treated like the crown fucking jewels. The airline *cannot* lose a bag with a gun in it. That would cause international-level pandemonium. Your suitcase will be tagged and carried, by a human, to the hold and then taken off the plane very carefully and handed to you at the baggage carousel by a nervous employee.

This is just the tip of the iceberg. There are hundreds of little hacks and shortcuts you can employ. You just need to have the chutzpah and the time to put in the effort. And once you're there, and once you know exactly what you can get away with, you can start to have a little fun. Now that I'm a fully established JewJetter, I've had untold adventures on aircraft. I don't bother walking all the way down the aisle to fuck anymore. What's the point? I'm in first class; I just happily hump right there in my seat. I'm not obnoxious about it. I don't flaunt it. I just mildly fuck. I'm as discreet as I can be in that situation, and most of the time no one cares and the crew won't intervene. If they do, I stop. Or come, depending on the time frame.

I once nearly brought about an emergency landing over Mongolia, en route to Seoul, when I plugged a hair straightener into my seat and took out the power for the whole cabin. Have you ever been on the plane when all the lights have gone out? Not that "It's nighttime so we're going to dim the overheads for the duration" sort of out, but an audible clunk and electrical fizzle and sudden pitch darkness. People do not accept that situation with calm, good grace. They panic. Especially when they are Korean (as these testy people were). They realize they are in a fragile metal tube flying through the air at high speed. And once the power comes back on, they all hate the schmuck looking guilty and holding the hot tongs. It's all right for them! They're Asian! They don't have to deal with the horrors of a Jew-fro after a lengthy flight.

This is all just JewJetting 101. You've just completed day one of a course that could possibly last for the rest of your life. The airlines keep evolving their systems and changing their approach. But I'm inside their heads. I know more about their industry than they do. I know every acronym and every line of lingo. I know what all that shit on your ticket means, what all that crap on the side of the plane stands for, what every mystery announcement made over the intercom translates to. As a passenger, I've mastered and surpassed them all.

There is only one unanswered question when it comes to me and my infinite knowledge of all things flying: Why the fuck don't these numbnuts hire me as a consultant?

CHAPTER 6

COMPLIMENTARY: MY OTHER FAVORITE C WORD

OK, let's start off this chapter by reading an e-mail together. Won't that be fun?

Mitchell,

I haven't seen you since our first day, but I wanted to reach out and thank you for making such a great impact on our stay. Despite the horrible weather, we've had a truly great experience, which has exceeded my expectations as a loyal Platinum member: your staff is second to none.

Unfortunately the hot-water outage came at a pretty poor time for us, as I was prepping for my

Saturday meeting and my partner was showering after
the gym. I understand these things rarely happen, and I
certainly appreciate the chocolates that were delivered.

We are leaving for the airport tomorrow morning
at nine. I'd like to know if you'd be willing to arrange
your house car for a final send-off back to frigid New
York as a gesture of goodwill. I am aware you have just
one car on the property that's in high demand but was
hoping you'd be able to honor this request in light of
the cold shower we had to endure.

Best regards,
Justin Lee

Pretty straightforward, right?

Wrong. This e-mail contains subtext, innuendo, and veiled
threats that may not be immediately apparent to the average or
slightly slow reader but will be screaming alarm bells to anyone
in the hospitality business. Now we are going to dissect this
e-mail and unearth what it's really saying.

"Mitchell . . ." OK, so who are we talking to here? Mitchell is the operations director of a property that is truly one of
the wonders of the hotel world. Unparalleled views of the city,
luxury oozing out of every orifice, and a level of service I have
never encountered anywhere. Orgasmic at every juncture. But
that doesn't mean I won't try to squeeze a few more drops of
goodness out of them, like they were my own nads after a long
weekend in Miami.

So Mitchell is almost at the top of the tree. Slightly above
him is the general manager, who was also cc'd on this e-mail.
You always need to know who can get things done at your
accommodation of choice and the management structure at the
organization. You don't hit up the head guy immediately. Aim
a little lower by trying to select someone that can be exploited,

but make sure the top guy is aware of your complaint. That'll make his underling feel like they have to act, just in case their boss is a close personal friend. I use "Mitchell" rather than "sir" or "Mr." to maintain a level of friendly interaction. Start off too formal, they are going to think you are really pissed off and it might make them instantly defensive.

"I haven't seen you since our first day, but I wanted to reach out and thank you for making such a great impact on our stay." Instantly, compliment sandwich. He will recognize this as a positive missive. Plus I threw in the fact that we had met when I arrived. Even if he doesn't remember me, it highlights my status. And getting what you want is all about status and the reinforcement of status. If you're identified as a schlub, you're getting nothing. This guy wouldn't meet every guest oozing through the front doors, but I was someone he was expected to meet. Someone notable. And I make sure he knows that I appreciated his importance and the positive effect it had on my life. Suddenly he's feeling all warm and gooey inside.

"Despite the horrible weather, we've had a truly great experience, which has exceeded my expectations as a loyal Platinum member: your staff is second to none." The vital words in this sentence? "Platinum member." OK, I'm a high roller. I'm spending seventy-five-plus nights in his brand's beds, and I want him to know it. If I'm some no-name from Arkansas he never expects to encounter again, I'll probably get brushed off. But I'm someone who attends and spends regularly at partner properties around the world. Again, it's a reiteration of my status. And as far as he's concerned, I'm happy hot shit as of this point in the letter. All was superpeachy with my stay. The inherent warm fuzziness continues. However . . .

"Unfortunately the hot-water outage came at a pretty poor time for us, as I was prepping for my Saturday meeting and my partner was showering after the gym." Now comes the hook.

I've buttered him up, and now it's time to take him down. There certainly was a hot-water outage at the hotel during my stay. However, it didn't affect me in the slightest. I either slept or boned through it. But I'd heard someone mention it the next morning at breakfast and knew I could sway this vital nugget of information to my benefit. Of course there was no Saturday meeting, except between my schlong and my female companion. And she indeed became sweaty after that particular workout but had been nowhere near the gym. But this guy doesn't know that. As far as he's concerned, I had to try and land some huge account while looking like shit and thinking about my shvitzy bitch of a partner back in my room. And it was all his fault.

Notice the use of the word "partner." I could have said "wife" or "girlfriend," but "partner" is a beautiful term to jam in there. It's got a tremendous ambiguity about it. What could "partner" mean? I was hoping to install a vision of pissed-off, rich, bitchy gay guys in this manager's mind, who, after black chicks, are the last demographic you want to annoy. If they feel undervalued, they will let you know about it at a high and painful register with a lot of needless hand movements. Not what you want in your face. So I always go with "partner." It's all about the details. Moving on . . .

"I understand these things rarely happen, and I certainly appreciate the chocolates that were delivered." Again, I'm not attributing blame to anyone. There's no shouting or chiding. More compliments to cram into the sandwich. I had my opening compliment, my complaint, then the second compliment to sweeten the deal. Plus I wanted to acknowledge what they had done for me already. Yes, they'd sent some luxury bonbons to my room after making sure the front desk knew about the whole water situation and my inconvenience (laying a bit of groundwork there at the same time), but I didn't want him coming back to me saying, "I hope you enjoyed the chocolates," and fobbing me off with that. No way. That would never be enough. Chocolates? Fucking chocolates after suffering the personal indignity of a cold shower? Ridiculous. So I get that out in the open. You gave me this. It was practically an insult. I want more. OK, time to drop the boom.

"We are leaving for the airport tomorrow morning at nine. I'd like to know if you'd be willing to arrange your house car for a final send-off back to frigid New York as a gesture of goodwill." You don't beat about the bush. You don't say things like "anything that you can give me." That sounds desperate. You have to be specific. This is what went wrong; this is what I want. Obviously it has to be the right balance. If your foot got run over by the housekeeping cart, you don't just ask for a fruit basket. Likewise, if you were missing a single hand towel, you don't try to get comped for the whole stay. Use the appropriate amount of recrimination. But you get something.

Also, you need to say "as a gesture of goodwill," which, in the hospitality business, means "Don't bill me for this." If you've got a big, swinging dick and stayed in the Diplomat's Suite, they might think you don't care about another $300 on your tab. You make it clear that you ain't paying shit. And you use hospitality parlance so they know you're not some amateur just trying their luck. You got fucked, you know what you're doing, and this is what makes it right. The "frigid New York" line takes the edge off a little bit. You're being playful. This isn't a threat. You're not a monster.

"I am aware you have just one car on the property that's in high demand but was hoping you'd be able to honor this request in light of the cold shower we had to endure." Again, nice and light. You are not some ape throwing your shit out of the cage at a fat woman in a hat. You don't downplay the situation, but the mention of a cold shower reiterates your pain and your need for compensation in a way considered classy by all. No anger, no bitterness. You reveal yourself as someone who expects the best and did not get that. You are trying to be understanding and reasonable.

"Best regards, Justin Lee." Look, I'm about to explain to you how to thoroughly manipulate the luxury-hotel sector. I have to be somewhat anonymous. So I don't use "Justin Ross Lee," as it's too easy to Google. I use a generic e-mail and my pared-down name. There are a lot of Justin Lees in the world (especially in Asia). Only one Justin Ross Lee.

So there you go. A massive amount of information crammed into that brief, perfunctory e-mail. But what can it all mean?

**

My approach to hotels, indeed any situation where I'm expected to spend my own money, is simple: never leave a shekel on the table. If I have to spend any cash at all (which is not a situation I enjoy; I was bar mitzvahed, after all), I sweat, piss, moan, and cajole to make up the balance elsewhere. I want to check out with exactly the same bank balance as when I checked in. And there are myriad devious ways to do this.

So as you have discovered, loyalty is everything. Just like with air miles, if you aren't a part of some hotel-chain points system, you are a giant schmuck. You are continually wiping your ass on fifty-dollar bills and flushing them into the sewer. Points equate to cash. Except hotels are happier to part with them than with real money. If you get fucked over or under-served (and you will be, even if you have to conjure up these situations yourself), you can easily get points as compensation. Getting folding money out of them takes more work. Points on your card seem like a cheap way to get you out of their face. And these points can be used for upgrades, free stays, perks, and general pampering. Now, I don't care if I stay in a suite the size of a football field. I don't care if there's a truffle the size of a bowling ball on my pillow. It's not really about getting stuff. It's about playing the system and winning. That's what all of this is about.

But there are different ways to play the system, as I will illustrate. Yes, you get perks if you're a member of some hotel chain's loyalty program, but that also means you need to conduct yourself a certain way. If you're at some no-name establishment that you know you'll never visit again, you can act in a completely different manner. Like a tremendous asshole, basically.

So first, if you have status at a hotel—as in you are part of their "family" and get their newsletter and carry a dumb plastic card in your pocket—you need to work just a little bit smarter. Most hotel chains with a points program expect you to stay at their lodgings for a certain number of days a year, and if you start acting like a giant douche bag all the time, alarms will activate every time they swipe your credit card. As demonstrated by my e-mail, you need to have a certain level of decorum.

Remember, you are always staying at the hotel on business. Even if you conga-line into reception wearing a Hawaiian shirt and one of those hats that hold a couple of beer cans, you are still there on business. Two reasons. For one, you get treated better if they think your firm is picking up the tab. They want their money. If things get shitty on a repeated basis, then that company is likely to take their business and millions of dollars elsewhere, and the hotel doesn't want that. Second, there are codes out there, floating across the Internet, that can be used for employees of certain companies. Pepsi, IBM, Raytheon— they all have discount codes for their employees at certain hotels, and I just happen to work for them all. And it costs me about six cents.

How is this possible? You get a bunch of business cards printed. They cost practically nothing and have unfeasible power. I'm currently the social media director at PepsiCo Inc., while also the senior resources coordinator at IBM, and not forgetting the chief information officer at Raytheon. All thanks to Vistaprint. What do those job titles mean? Who gives a shit? They never ask anyway. But if they did, you give them a card. They aren't interested. There's bound to be some screaming kid or brain-dead yokel behind you at the reception line who's just stuck his dick in the outlet or something. The front desk wants you out of their life as quickly as possible. They aren't going to call Bethesda and get your credentials checked out. You can wipe hundreds of dollars off the cost of your room by doing this, and you still get your loyalty points at the end of it on top of all that. Just for a business card and a little white lie. But, obviously, that is not enough.

Now that you have the reduced cost of your room (thanks to your company discount code), you can start to work on making up the difference. Remember, you need to be done when you walk out of that place, having spent absolutely nothing. Say you've got the price of your room down to $200 a night. You have to ensure, against all odds, that you get $200 of service out of that hotel on a daily basis. My ride to the airport, courtesy of the property? What would that be worth? A hundred dollars? Maybe more? That gets added to the total.

Shoe shines, luxury toiletries, meals, drinks in the executive club lounge. Anything they are offering for free you grab and you hang on to in order to restore the financial balance. It all slowly erodes the cost of your room. And once you've taken advantage of the legitimate stuff, you start to look for problems. And there are always problems. Hotels are built on problems. Look hard enough, and you'll find something wrong with your room or the elevator or the hallway. Something dirty, something broken, some weird noise, some strange smell. Call down to reception. If they don't answer? Great! Use that against them as well. It's almost impossible for them to confirm that someone didn't answer your call. Their fucking phones are ringing constantly. So once they answer, you release an exasperated "finally" and tell them it's the fourth time you've tried to reach them.

Does your room come with a complimentary breakfast? Then you eat the fuck out of that thing. Order any bespoke item they offer. And if they don't offer it, insist that they offer it. Tell them you have some dietary restriction that means you have to have lobster four times a day. Do you think they'd argue with that? And then try and get lots of wine out of them. Hotels just love to give out wine. Just remember how much that costs, and knock it off your grand total. At some of the more high-end establishments I've stayed at, I've had $150 to $200 breakfasts every single day! I've camped out in the breakfast restaurant until midafternoon! Deviled eggs with caviar, truffle omelettes, smoked salmon, champagne—if they have it lying around, make sure it gets in your mouth.

And once in your room, call down for sodas or snacks or chocolate. Examine the room guide and the room-service menu carefully. Do they give you free Fiji water? Get extra free Fiji water. Coffee machine in the room? Stock up on java to take home with you. Luxury bathroom products? Ensure you get a fresh set of everything every day. Don't leave that Bulgari shower gel in the tub like a schmuck; place it in your luggage and get another one the next day. And if you don't, let them know and see if the management will comp you a drink for all the pain you have suffered. And if they give you a free-drink token, make sure your "partner" is given one as well. Get your valet parking comped by inventing some bullshit vehicular discretion (never park your own car, and never pay for the privilege). And make sure you inform them of all this on site. They are more likely to respond to problems as they are occurring than when you're just a distant memory who's left hard-to-remove stains on their sheets.

Having a working knowledge of the hospitality-business lexicon really helps as well. It disarms them. Suddenly you're not one putz, but a potential hotel expert. So you never have a "problem"; you have a "service failure," which requires a "ser-vice recovery." Once they hear terms like that, they know they are dealing with a pro. You're a seasoned traveler or someone who is in the business. It scares the shit out of them. "Managing expectations" is another phrase that helps to tighten their sphincters. If they didn't "manage or meet your expectations"— and even if they did—they need to pay up. "Transparency" also strikes fear in their hearts. I had the upper echelons of a hotel in Tokyo almost hara-kiri when I informed them they had not been "transparent" when it came to my expected window view of Mount Fuji and they should be ashamed of themselves. They eventually put me in a room that was so large it had its own business center that I didn't even find until my third day in there. Easily one of the most exclusive and expensive suites on the planet. Just because I dropped "transparency" into the conversation (and made them feel traditional Japanese shame).

Likewise, a working knowledge of the important job titles is essential. These tend to change from hotel to hotel, though the chain of command is usually the same. There should be some sort of directory in the room, where you can get the general manager's name and the titles of his underlings. Top dogs love splashing their signature all over everything. If you can't find the directory for some reason, just call and ask. Make up some bullshit about you wondering how best to reach out to the general manager to compliment a member of his staff. Find the most empowered weakest link. Know the pecking order and use it to your advantage.

And if you start to feel bad about all these cost analyses and free martinis, don't forget, they are in the business of thoroughly bottom-line fucking you. Like any business, they want to fuck you and take your money. All you are doing is lightly penetrating them back. No one is dying here. The Hiltons are not boarding up the windows tomorrow. We've gone through a global financial meltdown of historic proportions. Do you remember any hotel chains going out of business? Of course not! Hospitality is a beautiful fucking racket! Lots of their staff are on minimum wage, and as long as there's a clean towel and no dead hookers in the beds, most people are happy. So don't feel sorry for faceless corporations.

Now I'm so used to pulling this sort of shit, I've started to get creative. And by creative, I mean freaky. For instance, I like to raid the minibar, as any healthy, red-blooded American does. Which is why I always travel with a clear nail polish (to reseal vodka bottles once they've been emptied out and refilled with water) and a lighter (to do the same if they have plastic seals that can be warmed and molded).

But I also enjoy leaving my calling card. I take the hideously overpriced, oversized Nestlé Crunch bar from the fridge, slide off the paper sleeve, delicately peel back the foil, take an X-Acto knife or razor blade, and carve away the center of the chocolate, to leave a frame of Crunch that I can refoil and then slide back into the wrapper, making it look like there's a complete bar in there. The next drunk dumbass that is desperate for some sugar will find their candy has been chewed away seemingly by termites. It might appear lightly demented, but consider it an ode to situational comedy. Like my hero, Frank Abagnale, you leave something behind.

If you are staying at a place where you have zero status, a total hit-and-run joint you never expect to bother again, you can have a whole new level of fun. By which I mean you can go completely fucking nuts. Which leads us to Operation First-Class Glass.

First-Class Glass

Not everything you do has to be a skillfully manipulated or a masterly contrived plan that Machiavelli would be happy to scrapbook later. Sometimes you just need to get down and dirty. And this little maneuver is definitely both.

You approach the no-name hotel that *you will never visit again* (I can't stress that enough). You check in. You say nothing. You don't try anything. You're just staying there in your role as a normal human being with no obvious defects or agenda. You go up to your room. You wait twenty minutes. Then you unwrap the ziplock baggie of broken glass that you brought with you. Sprinkle a few small but potentially damaging shards beside and slightly under your bed. Then you call down to the front desk.

"I need the front-office manager up in my room right now. This is an emergency. This is a code-red grievance . . ." Etcetera, etcetera.

Don't tell them what the problem is. Just make sure they know there is a problem. And that you are pissed.

When they arrive, you'll be on the phone. You'll be talking about your situation to an unknown caller, but not to them. As far as they are concerned, you could be yakking to your lawyer or the press or the TripAdvisor hotline. They don't know. But they will be hearing the details of your disaster as you emotionally reel them off to this unknown quantity, making them aware that you've found glass all over the carpet and your foot could have been shredded like coleslaw at a particularly uninspiring wedding buffet. An artery might have been breached. Nerve damage. Tetanus. You could easily have died.

Then you hang up and turn to them. You demand to know how this could have happened. You wonder what kind of two-bit fleabag of a shithole you've landed in. You make it abundantly clear how appalled you are and how ashamed they should be. How dare they? How dare they send you to your inevitable doom in this way? Yes, you lay it on thick. And they will be terrified. This is the last thing in the world they want. In most hotels, people suck it up. They absorb their problems and never say a word. And they get nothing as a consequence. But you make your feelings clear. Then you start to make your demands.

Obviously a new room for starters. Not just a similar room—a better room. A vastly better room. A room without glass or other life-threatening substances scattered all over the place. (You're allowed to be a little condescending after the trauma you have just encountered.) And possibly a few free drinks to calm your nerves. Or a bottle of champagne to celebrate the fact that you are still alive. You need to gauge your gouging by the desperate expressions on the faces of the staff before you. If they look like they are about to cry or throw up, you can push it a little further.

I pulled the glass trick at some fairly luxurious place in Michigan. Why was I in Michigan? I have absolutely no fucking idea. Maybe I lost a bet or murdered a nun in a former life. But there I was, knowing I'd never ever ever go to this particular hotel again, so it was the ideal venue to try the glass trick. Which I did and wangled a massive suite, plus a $300 F&B credit, and had the entire staff by the pussy hairs for the rest of my stay. If I'd wanted my ass wiped, I would just have to look at the reception staff in the right way and they'd come running with a rag.

All of this for the price of a few shards of broken glass. Now, I know people try similar things with condoms full of moisturizer and shit like that. But they've copped to it. Plus, unless you suddenly start guzzling on that stranger's jizz, there's not much bodily damage that can occur from a used condom. But broken glass can have a far more dramatic effect on your body and their Yelp rating.

Now, I know exactly what you pussies are thinking. "Oh, the poor minimum-wage salt-of-the-earth people who scrimp and scrub all their lives only to have a prick wander up, start hurling chunks of glass around, and get them hurled onto the scrap heap of life." Look, I'm interested in fist-fucking the Hiltons (some of them are used to it) and their ilk. I'm engaged in a psychic war against any corporation that would insult their guests with a "resort fee." But I don't want to damage civilians. Collateral damage should be avoided at all costs. That's why you always confess.

Again, I can't make it clearer: you don't pull this shit at any establishment that you're ever planning to return to or have any level of status at. These are places you can walk away from while flipping the bird and screaming various fuck-yous at any sundry staff. So you own up to your little trick. But you do it in your own way. Firstly, when you check in, don't give these dildos your credit card details. That can easily be traced back to you, and once they have a means of getting at your cash, they will get at your cash. Just make up some shit about your card being stolen or your being Amish or something like that, and then offer to give them a cash deposit instead. They might look at you like you're some sort of deviant, but they will usually be happy to take your shekels.

Then, once you've glassed and upgraded and gleaned anything else that's coming your way and you are about to leave, you write a letter and address it to the head of housekeeping or similar. Leave it on the nightstand (or mail it from a safe distance if you're nervous), and flee, grabbing your cash deposit on the way out. In the letter you say some dumb shit like "Look, I fucked up. I realized afterward I'd broken the glass myself; something splintered in my luggage, and I didn't realize until later, and I was too embarrassed to say anything . . ." Get Conchita off the hook, leave her a big tip, and you'll be able to sleep soundly at night.

I appreciate it's not a sophisticated swindle suitable for use as the plot to *The Sting 3*, but it gets you where you are going. Remember, never leave a penny on the table. You leave with as much cash as you arrived with. And sometimes you have to act like an asshole to achieve that. Some of us find that easier to accomplish than others.

CHAPTER 7

BJS, DJS, CHAMPAGNE, AND SLUTS: SKIPPING THE VELVET ROPE

The two dirtiest words in the nightclub business are not, as you'd expect, "bathroom whore," but rather "revenue customer."

It must be the only industry on the planet where people who actually spend money are considered the enemy. But they are. They are seen as schmucks who are completely exploitable and so completely worthless. No one should pay seventeen dollars for a watered-down vodka soda in a small, sweaty room where it's impossible to breathe or conduct a conversation, civilized or otherwise, but they do. They're happy to pay an extortionate entrance fee and even more extortionate bar prices while the pros laugh in their faces. Fuck knows why, but the idiots keep coming back for more. And that makes them a target. They are the fodder of the nightclub world, leeched upon by bar staff, dance-floor skanks, and assholes like me.

I can see him now. The perfect mark. Overweight, sweaty, desperate. Wearing clothes that cost a shitload of money but exuded no style at all. Like everyone, this guy was there to fuck or get fucked. That's what nightclubs are all about. There's no romance to it. No hidden agenda. They are not designed for music fans or cocktail aficionados. They exist solely for the purpose of fucking. For people to meet and shtupp or at least have the chance that eventually shtupping will occur. So individuals who are completely incapable of hooking up with vaguely attractive women can hopefully facilitate hooking up with vaguely attractive women.

In that state, these people are vulnerable and easy to manipulate. It's not nice, but they're not nice. If they had a shred of decency within them, they wouldn't be in this grim situation, buying their spot at the best table in the club, blowing thousands of dollars on bottles of liquor, and attracting hot girls like puke attracts a hungry dog.

On this particular evening, I had just spotted the ultimate revenue customer. My quintessential vision of a mark, conspicuously perched at a table in the middle of Pink Elephant. He caught my eye the second I entered. Other guys look around the room for hot girls to home in on as they enter a nightclub. I look for the putzes. And this putz had a really good table. Prime real estate. Which means he must have dropped a lot of dough already. You don't get a table like that through chance. They won't allow it. The only way someone who looks like that gets a decent table in a club like that is by throwing down some heavy-duty cash. He was wearing a dark shirt that was already starting to stain at the pits, a suit that was too small for him, and a dumb tie dragged halfway across his neck. I fucking hate ties. That might be the reason I chose to rip this fucker apart like a shark through a stoned surfer. Something about him really irked me. So I decided to irk him back.

My guess was he was in finance and he had got lucky. Or some computer nerd who had off-loaded an algorithm for an eight-figure sum. Whatever he was, he had no idea how to deal with women. The typical club girls who were already hanging off him looked vaguely bored and were talking to each other while he grinned at them like a masturbating chimp.

I make a habit of qualifying guys such as this for fuel. Paying for my drinks, allowing me access to women, finding me a nice seat. It is all too easy to get inside their heads, befriend them, and convince them it is worth their while to be in your intimate circle. All you need is an in. Usually I use a female. Some smoking-hot piece of tail who can rub up against them and get their attention. They chat to this douche bag, introduce me, and away we go. Within seconds I'll be working him like a Muppet.

But that night I was working alone and had a much better piece of ammunition to use. Someone I knew who would impress the fuck out of this poor, unfortunate turd and have him eating out of my palm. Three words that would get me a place at his well-positioned table and the opportunity to begin emptying his bottles.

Sammy fucking Sosa.

How did I know Sammy Sosa? How the fuck do I know anyone? He was a club rat like me. Considering he was supposed to be a professional athlete, he spent a lot of time out late and in the dark. I knew all the owners and the promoters, and he did, too. We moved in the same circles, got introduced a few times, and I kept him in my back pocket. I didn't give a shit about sports and had to Google him the first time we met, but knowing someone like that is always going to pay off. He's the perfect guy to whip out in this sort of situation and impress some no-name with too much money and a glandular problem.

So I wandered over to Sammy and screamed a few words of greeting, as is the way in this environment. We chatted, and then I told him, "There's a guy I'd love you to meet." Sammy was accommodating. He gets that kind of shit all the time. I dragged him over to my intended victim, who was currently being ignored by a tableful of hot girls, and said, "Hey! I'd love you to meet Sammy Sosa."

Obviously this guy was stunned. And wasted. Which helped him accept that a complete stranger was offering him Sammy Sosa's hand to shake. And Sammy, of course, is used to meeting drunken assholes on a fairly regular basis and chatted up this prick like a pro. They exchanged twenty words or so, took a picture together. Sammy shook my hand, left us, and then I smiled.

"Sammy fucking Sosa. Can you believe it?"

He couldn't, and we started talking about the unbelievable fact that I'd just introduced them. We laughed and shook our heads and smirked like idiots, and then this dunderhead offered me a drink.

Bingo, I was in. And once I was there, situated at his table, a fifty-dollar cocktail floating in front of me, I really started to go to work. I wanted to grind this guy's table into dust. And the best way to do that is through pussy. As newer, hotter girls walked into the club and by our table, I'd drag them over to join us. I knew them all, of course, and we all knew we were there to be used in one way or another. It's part of the game.

So more and more girls were joining us, each hotter than the last. Models, actresses, trust-funders, heiresses, airheads. Every fucking stratum of slut was making an appearance. And this guy's eyes started popping out of his head, even as he was slowly being edged to the far end of the table. In fact, soon he wasn't even at the table. He was on a chair *near* the table as I held court, ordering bottle after bottle of vodka or champagne or whatever these bitches wanted and charging it all to this guy. It was amazing. Soon he was silent and overwhelmed, unable to act as this insane Jew ran up his tab to NASA-like levels.

So what kept him hanging on? There was one girl there he was transfixed by. A brunette. Stunning. I'd banged her, obviously. She was fine—nothing to write home about. But this guy couldn't take his eyes off her. He kept leaning over, trying to say a few words to her. She was playing along. She was a pro and knew he was the breadwinner. And I'm sure she would have gone home with him if I'd allowed it. But I wasn't feeling charitable.

As the night reached its inevitable conclusion, I waited until he got the tab. And that is a joyous feeling, seeing some loser hand over his gold Amex and spend twenty grand or whatever it was on my night out. But that wasn't quite enough.

As he stuck his card into the slot, I grabbed the bitch he had the hots for and dragged her out of the club, right in front of him. He looked like he'd opened his Christmas stocking and found a severed foot inside it.

"Nice meeting you," I said with the utmost formality, and I took his fantasy girl out of his life forever. It was a dick move. I'm a dick.

There's another thing I love in these types of situations. It's the expression on my doorman's face as I bring some smoking-hot girl into the building at five in the morning for the fifth time that week. Despite his doorman's oath, he couldn't help but laugh out loud and shake his head at my utter fucking decadence. He'd seen me leave at midnight. Back at five with a skank. Like clockwork. Yeah, that makes me feel good, too.

***

The nightclub world has a complex, delicately layered infrastructure that revolves solely around pussy. Especially in New York. Nowhere is like Manhattan when it comes to clubs. It's like a perfect storm of debauchery. You have the money, you have the models, you have the late-night licenses, and you have the locality. Compared to many places, it's relatively tourist-free and pretty fucking incestuous. It's not a fucking cartoon like Vegas or Los Angeles. It has a history, a culture, and a personality. Although these clubs spring up and then die with alarming regularity, the same characters haunt them. Bouncers, doormen, waitresses, bar staff, bathroom attendants—they stay in the pool forever, moving on to the next place when their current employer bites the dust.

It has something of a family atmosphere, and like most families, it's completely dysfunctional. It's a bitterly competitive community, but also a really supportive one. If you can get on the inside (as I did), you'll never pay a penny, even as a customer. But getting to that point takes work. A shitload of work. You need to develop status. That fuels everything in the industry. Not money—status. Because to get laid, you have to prove to the girls concerned that you're worth it. And as I've mentioned, getting laid is what the game is all about.

I estimate that I have probably consumed around $350,000 to $500,000 in comped product and service during the height of my club-ratting existence as a nonrevenue customer. That's taking into account the extortionate prices they charge at every level. Getting in, getting tables, getting drinks—they overcharge consistently and maliciously. The dumbbells who pay are happy to pay, because they want to get laid. And they think the fastest way to get into someone's panties is through their wallet. There's an entire profession based on that business model, but for some reason they haven't encountered it. And let me tell you, it would be a lot cheaper to get a whore.

So financially, there are a number of idiotic, rich guys (and it is always guys) who support the whole industry. The rest of us just suck at their teats and work on our positions within the club. All we want to do is never wait in line. At the door outside, at the bathrooms inside, at the bar, at the tables— anywhere. The ultimate goal is to stroll up to a doorway, get the bouncer who is built like a linebacker to give you a hug, to get the guy with the clipboard to not even look down and just usher you in, to have a drink placed in your hand, and to be led to a table in the prime spot in the club that already has five beautiful women sitting there. And for many years, that's exactly what I did. And here's how.

You start with three clubs. Do a little research; find out where's hot right now. Don't focus on just one; you need to play the spread. And then you work them to death. Five, six times a week you'll visit one or two in rotation, getting your face known, chatting up the staff, befriending everyone you can find. The bouncers are the best people to get on your side. They hold all the power. You make them feel special, and they will do anything for you. Their entire profession is based on being treated like shit by rich, white, drunken pricks that look exactly like you. Show them some respect, and they will do your bidding.

When you're first getting to know a place, get your story straight and keep it short and sweet. This is your elevator pitch, which you desperately need to land to get you inside a club. Be confident and succinct. "I'm not on the list, I don't have a table, but I've heard you guys are great. I just wanted to grab a drink and see for myself. Can you accommodate me?" Usually they will be so taken aback by your candor that they'll snap that velvet rope open lickety-shit. Then, as you exit, you talk to them again. Thank them for their kindness; shake their hand. Get them to remember you so that when you hit the place again, they'll smile and usher you inside.

And if you try and fail, don't hang around. Clubs like to have a long line of expectant putzes salivating outside, desperate for entry. It makes idiots who are passing by think, "Shit, there must be something really fucking special going on inside there." There isn't. It's just a nightclub. They are all exactly the same. But you will damage the mystique somewhat if you're standing in the doorway, throwing a hissy fit because they don't like the look of you. Retreat and try again on a different day with different staff on the door.

When you're on the inside, you need to find the promoters and get them in your pocket. These are guys paid by the club owners to drag beautiful people to their establishments and keep them there. They are the dung attracting rich, stupid flies who will actually spend some cash. The promoters always have the best tables, the sweetest liquor, and the hottest girls clustered around them like genital warts. They are total douche bags but can be won over pretty easily with flattery. Few are smart. Throw a few kind words in their direction, and they'll be sniffing at your crotch like a puppy.

I'm happy to take their booze and their skanks. It gives me the same sense of sick satisfaction as watching my cleaning lady pick up a used condom. They are an unnecessary evil, there to dredge the last few shekels from any passing Persian with a lubricated wallet. But they usually have the prime real estate in the club, and from there you can work the rest of the place. That's why it's important to know the layout of the club you're trying to infiltrate. It's not just a bar, some tables, and a dance floor. This is territory we're talking about. And if you're at the best table, it will be assumed that you're a somebody. And from that position you can start to work on the other members of the staff. The waitresses, the busboys, the cleaners. Everyone can be exploited for your own ends. As you make your presence known, you'll soon be part of the family and enjoy all the advantages that offers.

Eventually you'll be recognized and accepted. And once you've fully integrated yourself into the life of the nightclub, untold wonders will be yours. You won't get the key to the executive bathroom, but you will get the code for the employee bathroom, which is even better. That's obviously the best location to bang broads and blow coke. The biggest financial loss of my entire nightclubbing career was the five-dollar bill I used to tip the Dominican guy who guarded bathroom four at Bungalow 8, which is where I'd drag any number of shiksas. And he'd only get that money once I'd sealed the deal. If I didn't get any, neither did he! But it still ended up costing me a fortune.

That's an important lesson in club life. If you start to spend money, you'll never stop. It's like fucking a woman and then handing her a thousand bucks. You're never going to get that pussy for free ever again. Once you've opened your pocketbook, there's blood in the water, and these fuckers won't rest until you're chum. Never spend a dime—that's the most important thing. Keep your legs open and your pockets closed. The best way to hang on to your trust fund is to forge and cultivate relationships.

Nightclubs are all about access. Access to doors. Access to booze. Access to holes. One to get you in and one to get you off. And the way you get both is to keep watching and learning. You know in the movie *Casino*? There's that quote from Ace Rothstein:

In Vegas, everybody's gotta watch everybody else. Since the players are looking to beat the casino, the dealers are watching the players. The box men are watching the dealers. The floor men are watching the box men. The pit bosses are watching the floor men. The shift bosses are watching the pit bosses. The casino manager is watching the shift bosses. I'm watching the casino manager. And the eye in the sky is watching us all.

It's exactly the same with club rats: In clubs, everybody's got to watch everybody else. The doormen are watching the bouncers. The managers are watching the doormen. The owners are watching the managers. The promoters are watching the owners. The bar staff are watching the promoters. And I'm the eye in the sky watching them all. And trying to fuck them all over.

The Full-Circle Approach

Sometimes, people are just assholes, and there's very little you can do about it. Especially the type of people who chose to make nightclubs their chosen career path. They have to be douchey; it's a vital part of the job description. And sometimes you can just get on the wrong side of them and stay there. But these situations can also be aggravated to your advantage.

If you are repeatedly trying and failing to get into a place and have run out of options, throw a fucking tantrum. Scream and curse and call the prick who is standing in your way every filthy name conceivable. Drag his mother and his pets into it. Question his sexuality or SAT scores. Edge the conversation to the point of violence, and then pull back. Say anything derogatory that springs to mind—just make sure that this schlub is going to remember you once the encounter is over.

Then you do something that no one expects. You apologize. Not there and then, but at a later date and at a neutral location. This may take a little bit of research and some trailing. Find out where they spend their off-hours, or unearth any other clubs they like to frequent. Approach them casually, as if it's a complete accident that the two of you are sharing the same space. Then you start with the soft soap.

"Look, I am disgusted with what happened the other night. I was completely out of line. I am having some personal issues at the moment, and I'm taking some pretty strong medication for an ongoing groin strain. I didn't mean to lash out at you. I was lashing out at myself. I am appalled by some of the things I said about you and your family. All I want to do now is make amends with you in some way. If there is anything I can do to make this situation right, just let me know. In the meantime, please understand how shocked and disappointed I am with myself."

Then you leave it at that and vanish. Don't try to elicit a reciprocal apology right there and then. You give it a little more time. But then you follow up with a gift. That's one of the reasons I got into the pocket-square business. It's the perfect compensation item for a whole litany of situations. So you send your victim a lovely present, with a note reiterating your regrets at your hideous behavior and your utter regret that it occurred. Wait a couple of days, and head back to the club.

Now they will do anything for you. You've shown humility. They will be so amazed that you went so far in your apology and were happy to make a complete martyr out of yourself that they'll allow you unfettered access to their grandmother's vulva if it was suddenly on offer. Yes, it takes a little legwork, and you need to make yourself look like a pissy little crybaby, but you're in! It works like a charm. And they'll never forget you. That's what I call the full-circle approach.

Now, this story is not exactly a prime example of the full-circle approach, but it does show you how any situation can be used for currency and leverage. It's been well documented that I have a complex and often dysfunctional relationship with many members of New York's nightclub elite. Once I started to get more famous and have more of a profile, I didn't need to wrangle or barter myself inside the velvet rope. I was JRL, and that was enough. But sometimes my actions had consequences.

As you may be aware, I had a run-in with Star Jones at a polo event in the Hamptons. I posed for a photo with her (of course) and then posted the picture featuring the both of us. Except that I had added a thought balloon next to Star's voluptuous head with the image of some Devil Dogs inside it. It was a cheap joke that got a lot of play on social media. It also got me banned from that establishment and anywhere else owned by Noah Tepperberg.

Despite being violently bald, Noah is a global bigwig, owning clubs and restaurants all over the planet, including Marquee, Tao, Lavo, and some more pretentious-sounding, bullshit places. He's an asshole, but he's a big-deal asshole and wields a lot of power. So he's not the sort of person you want to piss off. And he's a grudge holder, as I was to discover.

Noah employed a doorman named Rich Thomas, who is an even bigger asshole than his boss. Just one of those pricks who's given a clipboard and decides to swing it like Ron Jeremy's dong. It's the only bit of power that he has in his life, and he likes to let you know about it. I've had many run-ins with him, including making him number one in my "Ten Most Hated People in New York Nightlife" (I only made number three). This and various other indiscretions by me in his general vicinity have not impressed him at all.

I'd just JewJetted over from Los Angeles, picked up a few shiksas en route, and headed over to a club called Avenue, where Thomas brandished his clipboard of power. He was not too excited by my appearance and basically told me to fuck off. Now, I don't like being refused entry when I have a number of lovely ladies on each arm. It makes me look like a soft-dicked imbecile. So I told Mr. Thomas exactly what I felt about him, in particular how he was a disgrace to his race (he's African American) and how I was more black than he was. This was in front of all the bouncers, and if there's one thing a black guy hates, it's being called out on not being black enough in front of other black guys. But then again, who does? Look, I know it wasn't classy, but honestly, this guy was an asshole.

So I left with my entourage and headed to 1 OAK, which is where everyone always washes up at the end of the night. It was a bit early for me to be there, two in the morning or so. I was casually having a drink with my party, standing near the bar, and minding my own business. So I was quite surprised to see Rich Thomas himself strolling over the dance floor and heading straight toward me at quite a pace. I couldn't believe he would have left his post at Avenue with such reckless abandon. I then realized he was obviously coming for me.

Which he did. He walked up and sucker punched me right in the gut. My indiscreet words in the doorway had obviously hit home, and he was seeking vengeance street-style. I could completely understand. But Rich had royally fucked up. Unfortunately for him, I'd just invested in a Flip cam that day to chronicle my exploits and had, partly by accident, managed to film the entire incident. I was surprised as he was, but I still pointed this out to him.

"You stupid dipshit, say cheese," I told him, pointing out the blinking red light of recrimination.

Rich looked like he had just crapped his pants, then grabbed the camera and ran off into the night. Now, this really pissed me off. First, because I could have posted that footage to YouTube and made him look like even more of an asshole and gotten a few hundred thousand hits. And also because I'd just got the fucking camera and it cost a couple hundred bucks. Getting punched is an occupational hazard for an asshole like me, but losing personal property is another thing entirely. So, on advice, I called a friend of mine who is a detective at the NYPD. (Which is a very useful ally to have. Take my advice: get yourself a friend at the local police department.)

My cop companion told me that Thomas was neck deep in shit. This was felony robbery, and even if he had a completely unblemished record, he would be arrested and charged and maybe jailed pending bail. Thanks to the cost of the goods, he had really fucked up. His cheap doorman outfit could be exchanged for a nice orange jumpsuit really fast.

I let all this information filter down to the media, the whole thing getting reported in a number of blogs, and eventually Rich, Noah, and his people got to hear about it. Soon I was summoned to a summit at Hillstone with Mr. Tepperberg's lawyers. They treated me like a long-lost brother, showering me with expensive cocktails and overpriced entrees and flattering me widely while alternately begging me not to press charges. They knew the shit it would cause them. There followed another meeting with Rich Thomas himself, where he had to suck up to me in a fairly unpleasant way. Which was fantastic.

I agreed to drop all the charges and forget about the whole thing. In return I was reinstated at all of Noah Tepperberg's establishments in perpetuity. And obviously, I never stepped foot in one of his places ever again. I wouldn't darken their towels with my presence. But I just wanted them to know that I could walk into one of his businesses and act like an asshole with complete impunity. Having that hanging over their heads was enough compensation for me.

And the lesson here? Any situation can be used to your advantage. By being an asshole to Rich Thomas, I was able to have the biggest nightclub owner in Manhattan treating me like a juror. Oh, and always film everything. That really helps.

CHAPTER 8

SHTUPPING ZUCKERBERG: HOW FACEBOOK RUINED MY LIFE

I'd fucked around with employment before, but this was my first real job. My first foot on the career ladder. My first job title that actually meant something. Not that it meant anything, obviously. It was a job title. They never mean anything.

But, remarkably, I was about to use my MBA talents in an administrative capacity at New York–Presbyterian Hospital at Columbia University, one of the most esteemed medical facilities in the country, if not the world. Obviously I'd landed this role through nepotism rather than through any skill on my part. My dad worked in the medical field, and he'd pulled a few strings to get me a job that I was completely unsuited for. It's the American dream.

So it was from this inauspicious vantage point that I dressed up to the proverbial GQ and headed way, way, way uptown for my first taste of the dreaded nine-to-five. Or, in fact, the eight-thirty-to-six.

At first it was quite exciting. I was given an ID and handed a catalogue of office supplies and equipment and ordered to pick out what I needed for the job and introduced to the gals in the typing pool and all that shit. Then I was shown to a "hot desk," where a huge pile of sickening manila files were placed in front of me. My boss said, "Good luck," and I was left alone. It was at that moment that I realized I had, in a George Costanza way, absolutely no fucking idea what I was supposed to do. None.

This wasn't just initial confusion on the first day of a job in which everything would work out once I got the hang of it. It was utter fucking confusion at even the basic fundamentals concerning my employment. Nada. I flipped through the paperwork, saw spreadsheets and graphs, and realized I was completely out of my element.

I was too dumb, proud, or paralyzed with fear to ask anyone for help. What was I supposed to ask? "Excuse me, can you tell me how to do my job?" This was what I'd had years of expensive college and graduate school to learn. Exactly this kind of MBA stuff. And it instantly struck me that I had no idea how to do it. Higher education is great at teaching you about things. Really crappy at teaching you how to do things.

It was then that it struck me. I did not want to work this way. Ever. It was horrible. The cold, sterile drabness of a medical facility with the sound of nervous typing and hushed conversations and trips to the pisser to break up the day. Fuck, it was scrotum-shrinkingly depressing. Everyone and everything around me was ugly. The walls, the faces, the furniture. It was an absolute avalanche of misery. I would have bolted for the exit right there and then, but my parents would have instilled

Jewish guilt within me. Dad had played many rounds of golf to get me here. I was ready to quit by eleven thirty.

So, with absolutely nothing to do, I started to post things on Facebook. I began to disassemble the working environment around me, pointing out characters, making up a few incidents, throwing in a few zingers, and generally bemoaning the shitstorm I presently found myself in. This was in the early, early days of Facebook. I don't even think the Like button had been invented yet. But people started to respond to my stories, asking for more detail, egging me on.

Obviously I loved this attention and gave the people what they wanted. I talked about how fugly the nurses in the hospital were (I thought nurses were supposed to be hot) and how I'd rather bang one of the cadavers than go anywhere near any of the staff with my dick. I jokingly mentioned licking all the tongue depressors and putting them back in the jar. I talked about how lame my boss was. And, of course, I constantly talked about how I had no clue what the fuck I was doing.

That was day one. I arrived on day two to discover my previous work space was now occupied. "We need somewhere to put you," a harassed administrator told me. "Let's have you work in here for the time being."

They set me up in an incredibly plush doctor's office. Big oak desk, bookcases filled with medical journals, huge leather chair. You get the picture. This was great. Something else I could offer to my audience. After one day of doing nothing, I could tell my Facebook friends that my brilliance had been recognized and suddenly I'd been promoted and here was my beautiful, grandiose office to prove it.

I needed the perfect picture to show off my achievements. I spent hours—*hours*—setting up my camera, balancing it precariously on a pile of anatomy manuals, then lounging in a chair with my feet up on the desk, looking like Gordon Gekko post–blow job. It was magnificent. But I just couldn't get the fucking thing looking right. I'd adopted my thousandth smug pose when my boss burst into the office and caught me floundering behind the desk.

"I thought I saw a flash going off in here," he said as I whipped my shoes off the surface and frantically tried to look like I was busy doing the thing that I was being paid for, whatever that was.

"Oh, I think it's these halogen bulbs in here. They're a bit flickery," I offered lamely, feeling like I'd just been caught pulling my pud at a funeral home. By some miracle he didn't notice the camera that was just out of his eyeline. He looked at me suspiciously and left.

Of course, I finally got the picture and stuck it up on Facebook, and people loved it. Lots of positive comments and encouragement. My growing audience wanted more. That was day two.

Day three began with a phone call. I'd been moved out of the office and onto another anonymous desk. So I was surprised by the phone ringing and assumed it wouldn't be for me. But by fuck was it for me.

"Justin, this is Dr. Berman." This wasn't my boss; this was my boss's boss. My sphincter tightened. If I'd been back in my old office, I could have looked up the medical term for that.

"Some alarming information has been brought to my attention. I received an anonymous e-mail this morning containing various screenshots from something called the Facebook . . ."

At the time Facebook was still a novelty and your whole fucking bloodline wasn't on there bothering you constantly and asking you to play *FarmVille*.

"Did you talk about the appearance of the nurses working at the facility? And did you say that you tampered with the tongue depressors and returned them to their jars? And did you mention my looks and my abilities? And was there a photographic image showing you in a doctor's office, pretending to be a senior member of medical staff?"

Obviously I denied absolutely everything. I told him I'd been hacked (I might have been the first protocelebrity to use that excuse) and I had no idea what that stuff was and how sorry and ashamed I felt by the entire experience and that it would never happen again. It made no difference.

He pointed out to me how much trouble the hospital would get into if this information leaked. If there was someone *inside* the facility talking about the size of cadavers' dicks and the attractiveness of the staff and soiling the sterile equipment for a joke.

I was fired. I wasn't just fired; I was *fired*. In fact, I was lucky just to be fired. I'd violated pretty much every clause in my contract in only forty-eight hours. I was immediately led off the premises. My ID was confiscated. In any discussion of the incident, I was referred to as an "intern." I was told that any items I had left on my desk would be shipped to me at a later date and under no circumstances could I ever enter the building again.

As you may have guessed, my parents were less than thrilled. In only two days, I had destroyed not only my career prospects, but also my father's relationship with hospital cronies. And, if it were possible, I had disappointed them even further.

It seemed I had acquired my first hater. Someone had seen what I'd been posting on Facebook, taken offense to it, and taken the trouble to record it and send it to my employers.

And if I knew who that anonymous whistle-blower was . . . I'd fucking hug them.

***

I knew what I wanted to do. I wanted to entertain. All I needed was a platform. But after this workplace debacle, I realized I had a captive audience right there on Facebook. They responded to the shit I put up there. They loved it or they hated it. And, to be honest, I didn't care which way they fell. I just loved generating material and getting a reaction from it.

I realized that this was a whole new way to broadcast. My followers and my reputation slowly grew. I understood the power of the words I was posting and the effect they had on people. It was a gradual learning curve. Having an idea, posting it, seeing how it went down. I'd whittle and hone and target my material, trying to maintain the perfect level of outrage that tickled my fans and provoked my haters.

This was material that I was generating and I could control. It allowed me to perfectly develop the wider world's vision of me and then audit the responses. It was all one-way traffic. And once the comments and the abuse started to flow, I could direct that, too. I just kept stirring the pot, squeezing the last bit of energy out of everything I posted.

Facebook was the launchpad. It was from there that the New York blogs started to glean information about my increasingly outrageous life and churn it into news. That first blog post—which, like so many others, was along the lines of "Who does this prick think he is?"—was a defining moment. I was so proud. I felt legitimized. I didn't really know what the fuck I was doing, and obviously they didn't know what the fuck I was doing, but whatever it was drove people crazy. Which generated interest. Which increased page impressions. That kept them coming back for more.

It's a clichéd term, I know, but I was developing my "brand." The brand was JRL: this shiksa-shtupping, doorman-aggravating, nightclub-bothering, celebrity-badgering, Jew-Jetting prick. I started to exploit my Jewishness and my family and my girlfriends until the wider world was hooked. I considered myself a satirical social media commentator surveying the world around me from my ivory tower.

Once the blogs started to take an interest, the so-called news media, desperate to fill their websites and broadcasts with anything vaguely human, followed suit. I think the first was a local Fox News website post about me and my devious, unfathomable ways. The usual stuff. That's when I knew I had arrived. I'd crossed over from being of interest only to some no-name in his bedroom piecing a blog together to attracting an actual media organization with offices and parking spaces and reach suddenly taking an interest in my exploits. That meant something.

From there I delicately cultivated infamy. Creating or appearing to create something noteworthy, whether it was a run-in with some nightclub doorman or a JewJetting incident or a celebrity sighting, I made sure to leak it to the blogs. As other outlets picked up on the stuff, my relevance and my standing grew. And as I became more of a name, everything else became easier. Easier to get closer to celebrities, easier to be approached by news sites for quotes, easier to get into places to cause mayhem and generate stories of relevancy.

That's when I buried Justin Lee. That guy was dead. Too many Justin Lees in the world. Only one Justin *Ross* Lee. JRL rose from the slab like the fucking beautiful monster he was. Then I couldn't stop the snowball rolling.

It was a two-pronged attack. First, they couldn't fucking work out what I was. I was this unfathomable abomination: questionably affluent, but with no immediate indication of how I became this way or why I acted the way I acted. I presented myself as a celebrity. I was a celebrity. There just wasn't a pigeonhole to conveniently shove me in. That drove them crazy.

Second, there was the celebrity aspect. All the gossip rags and the tabloids (and, increasingly, the quality press) desperately want celebrity stories. They don't care who they are or where they come from. And I generated celebrity stories constantly. All I needed was a photo.

I can't overemphasize the power of a photograph. I loved doing a shtick on my Facebook page. I adored doing bits and writing material. But that was nothing compared to a single picture. Especially when I came up with the idea of adding thought balloons to the images (à la Star Jones with the Devil Dogs) and posting them on Facebook. Ride the tidal wave of coverage, hilarity, and abuse. Spin it out, with me claiming that Star's "people" were outraged and had me turfed out of the Hamptons polo scene. Have them deny it. Have me comment on the denial. These things could go on forever.

As long as I could get near a celebrity and get a picture, I could generate a story. And as I became more renowned, thanks to the stories I was generating, accessing the celebs and being at the events that they attended got easier. Then, once there, I could grab a shot of some actor or familiar face and anonymously leak some story to a gossip rag, who would then approach me for comment. It was beautifully double ended. I was a puppeteer, playing the celebrity-obsessed media at its own game and yanking everybody's chains in the process.

JewJetting really helped. I was able to get access to first-class cabins and lounges using my various aviation schemes. And that's the best spot to hit celebrities. They are usually away from their minders, they have their guards down, and they've probably got a couple of drinks inside them. I basically stalked the 4:30 p.m. United flight from LAX to JFK. That's the one all the celebs took. They weren't getting the red eye. They were on this one particular flight. And so was I. I'd just jet back and forth between Los Angeles and New York, spotting notoriety and grabbing a picture. If something notable happened, I sold the story.

I'm not proud of that. I realize it's utterly despicable. But I saw it as crawling my way up the ladder. It was the equivalent of a bimbo blowing a casting director to get a part. I'd sell out these celebs for my own ends. And they don't give a shit. It's all part of the business. They need the coverage as much as I do. When people stop talking about them, they disappear. It's a game and they know it. As I may have mentioned, celebrities aren't people.

And I got better and better. Better picture selection, better captions, more followers, more interest. As Facebook became this global phenomenon, it took me with it. I was known as a "Facebook celebrity" just as Facebook was entering everyone's consciousness. Then the "real" press took notice. Suddenly the *New York Times* was taking an interest and featuring me. That's when I became legitimate. The *New York Times* is the newspaper of record. If you want to dig up information about something historic, that's where you turn. And I was in there, messing up their pages. And even though they still had no idea what I was trying to do, it kept my parents off my back for a while. If I was in the *New York Times*, I must be doing something right.

And once I was in the newspapers, then television soon came running up to me and humped my leg. I can come up with great shtick off the top of my head and look good on camera, so I was perfect for rag-type shows. Plus I was easy to hate and make fun of. It was shooting fish in a barrel for them. You don't need a bank of top Hollywood writers to come up with some insulting remarks aimed at me. I was ideal for the reality-show circuit. As far as they were concerned, I was rich, single, and outrageous. Ideal fodder for their endless churn. More exposure translated into more notoriety and a further climb up the ladder.

Monetizing this was always difficult. I was projecting this vision of wealth and excess . . . on a shoestring budget. As I became more notable, things like personal appearances started to happen. Soon people were paying me thousands to show up at their nightclub and wave a champagne glass in their general direction. Then there were sponsorship deals and mountains of free stuff. It's a depressing truth that as you gain notoriety, you pay for less and less. The biggest stars on the planet could buy anything they want, but they don't have to pay for anything at all.

Soon people were paying me to be seen with them. Rich kids and millennials (my audience) would pay cash to have lunch with me or even just stand beside them as they got a selfie. A cult of personality emerged. I was a "legend," and fucks with more money than sense were actually willing to part with currency to rub up against JRL for a moment.

But I knew I needed some signature thing to help keep the coffers healthy. I think it was in 2010 that I had my eureka moment. Pocket squares. They are garish, luxurious, and have absolutely no function except to be decorative. The perfect epitome of me. Once I had that off the ground, all my appearances and stories would have a pocket square shoehorned in there somewhere. It was the perfect item to give away to wronged enemies and new celebrity friends. Someone would turn up on the red carpet peacocking with a Pretentious Pocket piece, and my sales would shoot up. It was ideal.

Plus it provided something for the press to hang off me. I was a "fashion designer" or a "haberdasher." Utter bullshit, of course, but anything to help the personification of my brand. And it meant I could be represented without even being there! They wouldn't just mention Pretentious Pocket—it was always

Justin Ross Lee's Pretentious Pocket. It was perfect. An arti-
fact that represented me wholly, which also brought in much-
needed cash flow.

Now I'm at the point where the thousands of followers and
millions of page impressions are having an adverse effect. My
notoriety has brought some celebrities to even shy away from
me. They know that a picture with them might translate into
some story in a tabloid somewhere, and they don't want the
aggravation. And then I have my own JRL clones, trying to do
what I do, replicating my style. They have no hope of getting
anywhere near what I do with as much originality, of course,
but it's flattering that they try.

Now everyone has figured out that saying controversial
shit on Facebook can get you fired. So, in a way, I was a pioneer.
One of the first to have Facebook "ruin my life." And I wouldn't
have it any other way.

The Millionaire Matchmaker *Mayhem*

This was an ideal showcase for my full set of media-manipulation
techniques. It had everything: lies, brutal exaggeration, misdi-
rection, anonymous tip-offs, and, thankfully, no one too clever
to deal with.

Now, I know that everyone likes their television to be completely escapist pap and aren't interested and don't like to think
about their beloved shows being entirely mired in bullshit. But
they are. All television is bullshit, and ironically, the reality
shows are the biggest bullshitters of all. They are so unhealthy
they should have a surgeon general's warning before each
airing.

So you won't be surprised to know that *Millionaire Matchmaker* tends to feature people who neither are millionaires nor

need to be matchmade. They are usually douchey guys with girlfriends at home, who look good on television. Some are instigators like me who are there to cause a scene and get into a fight with Patti that will look great in the promos.

I knew my role and was determined to play it to the hilt. What I didn't expect, until I'd passed through the audition and screening process, was how fucking cheap these people are. As you are playing the role of "millionaire," they actually assume you'll be happy picking up the tab for every fucking thing—the trips and the meals and the dates. The production company didn't want to put its hand in its pocket once. They expect you to foot the bill. So that was the first angle I had to work.

There was no way that I was spending a single dime on this fiasco. But I didn't want them to know that. So I played along at first. I borrowed a luxury uptown apartment from my friend Ben Richman and pretended it was mine. Went over there the night before the shoot and threw a few portraits of yours truly on the wall. The crew and producers were impressed. It really looked like I had plenty of fuck-you money to throw their way.

I told them I had a pal with a private jet that would be an ideal place for the luxury date that would be the centerpiece of the show. I made it clear that I was happy to organize everything and foot the bill. All I asked was, in case of some unforeseeable disaster, that they line up a plan B for me. Of course, they ate up the idea of a private jet. That would look really fucking good on camera. So they went along with it. While I sorted out the "jet," they had a yacht lined up in case it fell through, which I insisted would never happen. But of course that's exactly what happened. There was never a jet.

At the last minute, the plane exploded, or the pilot broke his pelvis, or the insurance company wouldn't cover it. Some total crap. I assured them we'd use their yacht and I'd sort out all the payments once we were through shooting. Which I had no intention of honoring, obviously.

By this time, my date had been selected. Of course you have this endless conveyor belt of skanks to pick from, displayed before you like you're some sort of sultan selecting the latest harem member but with a lot less class and hummus involved. But the producers knew who I was going to get. And I knew who I was going to get. Or at least which woman was shoved in my direction. I didn't actually know a single thing about her, but I was determined to find some dirt.

The full names of the girls are never disclosed to the millionaires on the show to protect them from contact in between shoots. But I knew there had to be a way to find out more. One of the production assistants had a clipboard with all the information on it, used to organize the shoot and arrange cars and that kind of shit. I pulled the old Pastis trick and knocked a glass onto the ground while we had a chat. As she was distracted by this, I took a picture of the clipboard with my phone and got all the information I needed.

I knew there was something fishy about my date (sorry to put that image in your mind), but I had no idea the depths of dishonesty I was about to uncover. A quick Google and ten dollars spent on a background check website revealed my date was not Canadian, as she claimed (very American, from the white-trash panhandle of Florida or something), was at least twelve years older than she said she was (well into her forties, though on the show she said thirty), and had changed her name on multiple occasions. But then there was the porn.

Holy shit, there was a lot of porn. I mean, none of it was that recent, and she looked a lot different now than she did back in her cinematic days (I think she got a little more work done with each divorce), but that was definitely her, sucking and straddling all over the Internet. I knew this was it. This was dynamite, and I had to use it. Before the show began, my plan was to have the top-rated episode of that season. And now I had a way to engineer this.

So now I was working the entire production to ensure I didn't have to pay for anything while I was there, working specific producers to make sure the message that I wanted to get across got across (I knew how these things worked, and you could be made to say anything in the edit suite, so I had to be so careful about what I expressed), and working my date so she didn't know that I'd uncovered her cum-gargling past. It was exhausting. But I realized if I played all these sides against each other and pulled it off, I would generate some unpurchasable publicity.

Timing would be everything, of course. I waited until our on-camera date began. We had our entrees, and then I dropped the bomb. I started innocently enough: "Listen, something has been bothering me. I need to mention it . . ." Then it all came out. Why didn't you mention that you're a veteran porn star that's had more pricks than a diabetic? I pulled out my phone and started watching a selection of her greatest hits right in front of her as the cameras rolled. I mentioned her Boobepedia entry, her interracial double penetration, and her impressive poundability.

I have never heard a TV filming location grow so quiet. Everyone was stunned. *Stunned.* The only sounds were audible gasps. She looked at me like the utter piece of shit I was, threw something at my head, then stormed off, screaming for her publicist. "Why would a porn star need a publicist?" I asked as she vanished into a stateroom. It was carnage. I said the word "porn" as often as I could during my bomb dropping and the subsequent interview. I wanted that to be the reason the date had disintegrated, but I knew Bravo would never air that. They have a reputation to uphold, and if it seemed like they were hiring any old hooker to appear on their show, then the franchise would take a hit.

So I attempted to guarantee that porn would at least be alluded to in the finished product. Afterward, completely sideswiped crew sidled up to me. They all wanted to see the evidence and watch this girl in action. I obliged, of course. The director, who said he'd been working on those types of shoots for decades, claimed that he'd never, ever seen anything like that in his entire career. It was pretty fucking fabulous television. Then there were all the OTF (on the fly) interviews, those sections where you talk directly to the camera and discuss how you "feel." Again I talked about my disgust at all the lies and said the word "porn" about a thousand times. All was going well. But I still had to face Patti.

Let me just sidebar for a second and say that Patti Stanger is not at all what you would expect. She is much, much worse. She is a monster. I won't even bother wasting my energy by listing her many inadequacies. But let me just offer some evidence. Even after eight or nine seasons, she still hasn't learned the name of anyone who mics her on that show. She treats everyone around her with total contempt. She doesn't eat or interact with anyone. The whole crew is equally terrified and appalled by her. She's just one of those people who you assume plays a terrible person and then turns out to be a terrible person. Just awful.

I knew I'd have a confrontation with her, because those shows are as formulaic as a rom-com aimed at the menopausal. The nice guy on the show gets all smiles and sweetness, and the other guy gets derided and shouted at. I was the other guy that week, so I knew I'd be throwing down with Patti. And I knew I had to get my zingers out there faster than her and make my mark on the show. Which, if you've seen the episode, you know I managed to do. Patti has a sharp tongue, but a dim mind. She was no match for me. And I appreciated that the whole inter-action would end with me storming, or being dragged, out of there, so I had to have the last word. I also planned to throw something at her. And just about the only thing you can throw at a woman without turning into Chris Brown is a pocket square. So I hurled a Pretentious Pocket beauty at her smug fat face with all the spite I could muster.

It was perfect. Got my pocket square featured in every promo and commercial for the show. My sales rocketed. After all the deception, the production company didn't dare invoice me for the date and all that other shit off the show. But my work still wasn't done.

I knew there was a good chance that Bravo would white-wash over all the porn stuff, but that was the story that the tabloids would be interested in. They couldn't give a shit about *Millionaire Matchmaker* under normal circumstances, but some filthy bitch pretending not to be a high-class hand pup-pet was sure to pique their interest. I just had to find a way to get the story out there. So, as I'd often done before, I became my own publicist. I contacted *Radar Online* and leaked the story under the promise of anonymity. They ran it and then contacted me for a statement. Class act that I was, I replied, "No comment."

So try as hard as they might to cover up the whole thing and claim I was upset due to my date lying about her age, the truth (as I saw it) finally got out there, and the legend of JRL grew even more girthsome. But listen, I have nothing but respect for the porno purveyor that I was matched up to. She was a player, just like me. I nearly met my match. I was just one step ahead of her.

CHAPTER 9

A SHIKSA A DAY KEEPS MY MOTHER AWAY

While I can imagine you'd think my deflowering was a momentous event involving fireworks, parades, and a new national holiday in Israel declared in my name, in reality it was pretty pathetic. Jewvenile, you could call it.

I had reached my sixteenth year as a bratty, obnoxious, incredibly Waspy Jew. As part of my birthright, I'd been shipped off to the West Coast to some SAT "cram camp" at UCLA, where other hideously privileged spawn of assholes assembled to study in a college-preparatory atmosphere.

I managed to bag the heiress of a pharmaceutical empire, which, considering the amount of chemicals I'd soon be shoving up my nose, was healthily ironic. Despite the extent of her bank balance, it was not exactly an enriching experience. More of a teenage fumble that resulted in my beautifully circumcised piece somehow entering her body. But it was over—that was the important thing. The stigma of being a virgin was behind me (and all over her back), and while it probably left the young lady in question slightly traumatized at the time, now she has a story to tell. She popped JRL's cherry. There's sure to be a statue or a ceremonial coin celebrating the event in the near future.

The problem was that once I had become a man, in the non–bar mitzvahed sense, I had no idea how to make it happen again. That unfathomable series of events that led to me getting some pussy appeared to have been achieved by voodoo. It was a total mystery. Try as I might with the shiksas in my suburb and at my school, I could not get anyone interested in my dick. Which, obviously, is a ridiculous situation.

It was only when I went away to prep school that things began to change. While I was renowned and infamous at Brewster, I was not popular, not in the high school sense. I wasn't a jock. I couldn't be pigeonholed easily as an instantly recognizable clique member. I was an obnoxious little prick who drove around in a golf cart and pissed off the authorities. While that may have occasionally got me a few nods of approval, it didn't get any female heads nodding in my lap, if you know what I mean.

Then one afternoon I was dangerously driving my golf cart across the quad when I saw a girl I had never seen before. She was a midsemester transplant, and she was remarkable. I nearly drove straight into a soccer tournament as she sashayed across my path. Holy shit, she was something. And I was smitten.

Her name was Jill, and every male member of the graduating class was trying to get into her pants. Freshmen, seniors, substitute teachers. Everybody wanted her. But she wasn't interested. She was too good, and she fucking knew it. But I had a plan.

At this time, I had the upper body and physical presence of a member of the Chinese gymnastics team. Buff I was not. Everything about me screamed "limp" except for my brain, of course, which is the organ I primarily used to nab this girl. It was then I realized how important it is to lay the groundwork. To "pre-close," as I would dub it years later. For reasons that I can only put down to having too much fucking money, Brewster Academy was one of the most technologically advanced educational facilities in the country at that time. Even though the Internet was in its infancy and YouTube was a twinkle in some nerd's ballsack, we had Ethernet ports up the yin-yang. We also had a rudimentary instant-messaging service ironically named FirstClass.

This is what I used to seduce Jill. We started exchanging sarcastic tittle-tattle that slowly grew more and more flirty. While I probably would have been tongue-tied and fiercely erect if I were talking to her in person, via instant messaging I could be witty, snide, and supremely clever. I slowly stripped away her defenses, and soon we were actually hanging out IRL, as I believe the millennials say.

But there was a problem. She wanted to fuck me. Now, I can probably imagine what your next question is going to be. But the reason this was a problem was because at dear old Brewster Academy, getting caught with a girl in your room was the worst possible offense that could happen. Blowing a line of coke off Subaru Sue's hatchback was less serious than having a late-night liaison with someone of the opposite gender.

But Jill really wanted to fuck me. We couldn't get off campus, and me getting caught in the girls' dorms was a horror I couldn't even contemplate. I'd be instantly expelled. So I had to get this chick into my dorm somehow. There were several things I had to overcome. Firstly, there was a security guard, Charlie, who patrolled the corridors looking for exactly the thing that I was attempting to do. Then there was Dean Doucheborn, who had a personal crusade against youthful sexual dalliances for reasons I can only imagine were sexual in and of themselves. He would drive around campus in his fucking Dodge Caravan with a flashlight, trying to track down any hormones running rampant.

I also had a roommate at the time. A glorious stoner named Will, who wouldn't be able to leave our room. There was nowhere to go! If he was caught wandering around the school in a pot haze while I humped, it would soon get back to me. So there were many hurdles between my throbbing schlong and the unknown treasures that Jill was concealing. It was a fucking pain in the ass.

But look, I may not have been actual JRL yet, but I was prototype JRL and I knew I could pull this off somehow. I started to plan this thing and work it like a military campaign. Cue Charlie, the security guard. Luckily I already had him in my pocket.

I didn't want to go behind his back, so I thought the easiest thing to do would be to tell him about the whole thing. And even though it would have resulted in his instant and painful dismissal, this fabulous asshole was willing to turn a blind eye so I could get my dick wet. It was fucking amazing. Not only would he ignore some teenage girl clambering into a dorm-room window; he actually helped me out with planning and strategic movements. He let me know when Dean Doucheborn would be turning the corner in his fucking minivan and about any other obstacles that may have derailed me.

With my roommate, it was just a case of straightforward bribery. I made him pretend to be the heaviest sleeper on the planet, where even the sounds of postpubescent exertion occurring a few feet from his head wouldn't rouse him.

And then, just to make sure there wouldn't be any further unpleasant surprises, I called in a fake emergency across campus. This was before the age of the omnipresent cell phone (which also caused havoc with the planning; I had to make sure the coast was clear the second she arrived, as I couldn't warn her of any disasters), so I had to use a far-flung campus pay phone, which wouldn't get traced back to me.

I knew I couldn't report anything too dramatic. A fire would have had the emergency services arriving and a full investigation taking place. No, I swung low and said that some kid I didn't know looked like he was having a seizure at a dorm that was on the other side of campus.

So it was with a distinct level of ass-clenching fear that I crouched by my window on the first night, waiting for Jill to arrive. Which she did, precisely on time. The plan went without a hitch. No nosy deans, no suspicious security, no wide-eyed roommates. It had been a huge, stress-filled undertaking, but it was on that night that I not only fell in teenage love with Jill, but also fell in love with the whole notion of pussy. It was all I wanted. And from that moment on, my life would be dedicated to the pursuit, and liberty, of all things pussy.

***

Of course it didn't last.

Incredibly, we had many dorm-based fuck sessions and were never caught. Not even close. And we carried on in this regard for a year or two—an eternity at that age. It even limped along when I left Brewster and went to college. But soon I knew things were going wrong.

The communication grew less intense; the gaps between calls got longer and longer. Soon they stopped altogether, and she just vanished. I was so pissed I took a car service all the way from Northeastern back up to New Hampshire and charged it to her account. When I arrived, I discovered she had a new me. Not so good looking, not so funny. But new and more easily attainable.

I was crushed.

But in a weird way, this heartbreak was a fundamental cornerstone in what became JRL. I moped around for a good three months, failing to eat, not going to class, acting like a jackass. Then one day, as I think all young men in my position do, I just said, "Fuck this." In my beleaguered state I threw myself into partying and one-night stands. And nothing perks you up more than those essentials.

So gradually I became a club rat. I had this smoking pad in Hartford, and I knew all the club owners, plus had the best coke in town. I threw myself into fairly free-falling hedonism. I'd drink heavily, blow my face off, go out to the clubs, stay up for two or three nights, and fuck anything decent with a heartbeat.

I wouldn't say, at first, there was any precision or technique connected to this. It was just a sort of dumb luck combined with a nihilistic abandon. I didn't care anymore. I'd had my heart crushed, so fuck it. But that was the curious thing: the less I cared, the more I got laid. And the more I got laid, the more my reputation as someone who gets laid grew. And once you're in that missionary position, you can pull off a little maneuver that gets you laid every single time.

This is what I learned in all my hours at clubs in Hartford. If sluts know you are a man whore (and I've never shied away from my inner man whore), they will want to try you out. And if you deny them that, it will drive them crazy. Here's what I started to do: There would be some piece of ass that I wanted to bang. I'd approach her, and I'd grab her hair. Not too hard, but I'd give it a tug so she felt a little pain and it got the endorphins rushing. Women love to have their hair played with; men don't do it enough. And if she tells you to get the fuck away from her and not to touch her hair, then she's not going to touch your dick.

So now you've got her attention. You start talking. Then you drop the bombshell. You say, "Look, I think you're great. And I'd really love to spend some more time with you. But listen, I have to make this very, very clear: you can come back to my place, and we can talk and have fun, but under no circumstances am I going to have sex with you."

And you leave it at that. You leave a little mystery hanging in the air. And this is going to drive her crazy. She knows that you've fucked her mother and her sister and all her friends and her fourth-grade teacher. But you've drawn the line with her. No matter what she was thinking beforehand, now there is no way that this woman is not going to find some way to fuck you. It's a situation where she thought she had all the control, but that was taken away from her. She desperately wants to get it back.

So you take her home and you play "just the tip." You tease her, just like you've been teasing her all night. You carry on insisting that this is all going to be purely platonic, until she snaps and fucks your brains out. That application of service denial has got me laid in every coastal state in the union.

Look, I am not claiming to be any sort of pickup artist, and this technique won't work for every cooze hound. But it works for me. As I mentioned, I'm a lucky fuck, and once your luck starts rolling it's hard to stop it.

And as this reputation grew, my confidence grew. It helped to bring out my inner JRL. Soon I was this guy who could talk to any chick in a bar, and I was really boxing above my weight class. Dime pieces were falling into my bed. It helped to have this character to rely on. When I was wearing the armor of

JRL, this invincible, arrogant asshole, nothing could touch me. Rejection was out of the question.

And the drugs definitely helped. Once I was high, I would do anything, no matter how crazy. The problem was I started to have more and more smoking-hot girls in my bed, but a limp dick in my hand. So I phased out the coke, but the confidence remained. I was JRL now. I acted like I *was* on coke all the time, but I didn't actually need it anymore.

And once JRL came into the picture and started to gain some notoriety, that was game over pussy-wise. Women just want to fuck JRL, under any circumstances. I was this disgusting, obnoxious, arrogant, privileged kosher pig. They thought there must be some hidden depths there to explore. Instead they just found more and more hidden shallows.

And then I started to realize the value of using women as props. Not only could they help you get into any club in town; they also enhanced my social media profile. Don't get me wrong, I could look at pictures of me all the time, but stick some beautiful girl with a beautiful cleavage hanging all over me, and the likes and the shares will grow as much as the semi-erect pricks checking out the image.

It was the rabbi's daughter who first tipped me off to this. Originally she was another one-night stand. But she was funny, and we started hanging out more and more until she became a full-time sidekick. She was great for generating material. This whole notion of the daughter of a rabbi shtupping the ultimate Jew was just too great. Soon I was on Facebook making gags about holes in the sheets and taking her up the kibbutz. It was perfect and got me a lot of shares and a growing legion of followers.

But the rabbi's daughter, and the various women who took her place, knew they were being used as props, sometimes without admitting it. They were always in on the joke. Plus they got to enjoy all that JRL runoff. The first-class trips, luxury lounges, the VIP rooms, the swanky meals, the hottest clubs. Even if it was all bullshit. We all have our price.

And speaking of price, it was because of this behavior that my inner man whore became an outie. I was contacted by a crazed JRL superfan. Incredibly she was also a rabbi's daughter (now this is the second I've shtupped), except her dad was some Israeli Orthodox superrabbi, with curls to boot. She'd gone off the rails and ended up, as many do, down in Florida. She was holed up at the Hard Rock Casino near Fort Lauderdale, where she'd lost a small fortune and couldn't leave until she'd won it back. Impeccable logic. She wanted me to head down there and spend some time with her.

Of course, I was appalled. Tickled and appalled. I told her how busy I was, how much money I would lose by schlepping down south, and how I couldn't be bought and sold. Which of course I can. We came to some arrangement where she would "reimburse" me for my time and all I had to do was act like her boyfriend for a few days.

It was demented, and $1,200 was agreed upon. I was flown down there and instantly installed in her suite. It wasn't even as if she were horrible looking. In fact, she had an incredible body. Her face . . . not so much. But when she put on the huge sunglasses that I insisted she wear at all times (even in the sack), she was definitely passable. I convinced her that constant shade wearing was all part of the JRL celebrity mystique. And, incredibly, she believed me.

I even "borrowed" her Mercedes for the day and took my ninety-five-year-old grandmother out for a joyride. I even brought her to eat at the casino, on my john's tab, of course. I adore my grandma and could never tell her that my surprise visit was completely funded by a rabbi's demented daughter who was paying me cold hard cash to plow her. That would be gauche.

And as much as I bragged to my pals about this whole situation and sent them pictures of this yenta who was giving me money in exchange for marital duties, I actually felt pretty grubby. After a couple of days, I wanted out. Of course, by this time she was completely in love with me. It all started to get a bit scary as she begged me to stay and made it clear that if I tried to leave, bad things could happen to me. I nearly had to call the cops to get me out of the situation. That would have been an interesting phone conversation.

Once this period of man-whoring was over, I realized the power of JRL. But I didn't quite understand just how far this reputation had stretched. And then I went to Sweden.

I'll delve into the international reach of the JRL legend elsewhere, but let me make a brief aside to discuss the merits of the women of Sweden. If you were not aware, Swedish women are the most sensational women in the world. Our nines and tens are their sixes and sevens. It is unreal. A nation of supermodels. And they love American men. If you can offer them something different, they will be all over you.

And there's nothing more unusual and alluring to beautiful Swedish eyes than JRL. In their socialist paradise, a conceited, self-obsessed, capitalist putz like me is irresistible. On my first trip, the second I stepped onto the tarmac from the plane, I was besieged by obscenely hot nineteen- or twenty-year-olds who grabbed at me like I was the Jewish Justin Bieber.

Before the trip, I'd chatted online with a few girls who promised me a good time when I got to their country. But the reality was far beyond anything I could have ever imagined. There were girls *throwing* themselves at me, each cuter than the last. I'd see chicks too hot for Victoria's Secret runway shows hurl vodka bottles at each other and engage in a full-on catfight in order to sit next to me.

And there were no games. No fucking around. It was all so practical. "What time can you get out of here so you can fuck me?" That sort of thing. There were no hang-ups. For a pussy hound like me, it was some sort of paradise. Too much of a paradise. I turned it into my own personal hell. I had to start saying no.

I was disgusted with myself, but after a few days of an endless conveyor belt featuring nonstop stunning shiksas, I was exhausted. In the past, when it was harder to get any, I would pretend to say no to get some. But now that I could have any chick in the room, I had to start turning it down for the purpose of self-preservation. I simply could not fuck anymore. And turning down the chance to violate a six-foot, blond Amazonian broke my fucking heart. But I guess these were first-world problems.

So I've had a certain amount of luck and a certain amount of brilliance. But now I know that if the pussy well ever did run dry, I could always move to Sweden and dip my bucket endlessly.

Of course, I was much more single then. Now I have the perfect ally in my darling Kate. If you've seen some Instagram photo of mine accompanied by comments along the lines of "Holy shit! Who is that chick with the impeccable rack?" that's Kate. The perfect JRL complement. A beautiful girl who is up for anything anywhere. Pack your bags in the middle of the night, and bring your passport—we're heading to JFK. Who knows how to play the game and accept my insanity. Here's a tip for you: get out there and find your own Kate. Except you can't. There's only one Kate. God, do I love her.

The Pre-Closing Technique

My initial seduction technique with Jill taught me many things. The most important was the power of groundwork.

Now, my powers both in person and via whatever electronic medium I choose to utilize are equally magnificent. But back in the early days, I was much more of a mensch when dealing with someone remotely.

Once I became a full-blown slut scout, I adapted this technique not only to save my precious time, but also to ensure a conquest. Rather than attempt to talk to a woman in a club with music blaring and assholes throwing beer on you, you'd get her digits with the promise to speak to her later.

Then you'd start an electronic relationship, casual at first. Just a few texts a week. Then you gradually increased the volume. You start to listen to her troubles. You gain her trust. You sympathize with the shit that's going on in her life (and there's always shit going on in a woman's life). And, most importantly, you make her laugh. You entertain her.

It's so much easier to control the flow of information and the topics covered when this is all done via text or e-mail. You might have trouble coming up with the perfect zinger when under pressure, but if you've got a bit of breathing space, you can provide a brilliant retort that illustrates just how great you are.

And slowly these girls start to imagine that they know you. You're in their heads. Then you can start to play a little. Suddenly they don't hear from you for a couple of days. They get nervous, get worried. Then you come roaring back, and they're relieved that you're installed in their lives once more.

After all of this pre-closing and flirtation, once you actually meet the person in the flesh, getting laid is guaranteed. Sometimes, at the height of my pre-closing powers, I'd be inside a girl within seconds of physically meeting her for the first time. And this maneuver is a great way to bag women who are way out of your league.

If you approach a completely unapproachable girl in a club or a bar, she can judge you within seconds and decide whether you are not right for her. But with the luxury of a prolonged session of virtual chat, you can convince her of what a stud you are before having to prove yourself.

It was by this method that I managed to entangle myself with an unbelievably smoking-hot thirty-eight-year-old. The textbook, dictionary definition of a MILF. Not that you see "MILF" in many textbooks or dictionaries. I was twenty-one or twenty-two at the time and had no right at all being anywhere near this woman. Not only was she married (to one of Hartford's leading bar owners and restaurateurs), possibly with kids, but she was so far out of my league, too, that we weren't even playing the same sport.

But I just began to ply her with positive reinforcement, the way a less reputable player would have plied her with roofies. I built up her confidence, constantly told her how magical she was, made her giggle, made her feel good, and then pulled the plug. She messaged and I didn't message back. Not for a few hours.

"What happened to you?"

I just fed her some bullshit line, but by then she needed me. Or felt like she needed me. I was offering her a bit of respite from her meaningless life. Once I'd started with the communication again, I had her hooked. Soon we turned the virtual into the physical, and she'd come over, do blow, and fuck my brains out.

She should have known better. She really should have known better. She was nearly twice my age, and I was playing her like a Jew armed with a calculator at a car dealership. But that just shows you the power of the pre-close. I went on to use this method many, many times with many, many shiksas.

And I wasn't doing anything bad. I was showering them with compliments. I was making them feel good. And I honestly did want to fuck all these people. This wasn't some sick power play. I really wanted to bang them, and, eventually, they wanted to bang me. No strings attached. They all had lives elsewhere. I just wanted to spend a little time to ensure I wasn't wasting my time.

Sure, it could be considered a little manipulative. But are there any other parts of a relationship that don't involve manipulation? I just did manipulation via text so I could be completely in control. So don't blame me. Blame my service provider.

CHAPTER 10

CLOCKING IN AND FUCKING OFF

Foolishly, in an attempt to prove something vague to someone vaguer, I decided to get a job. Not just any job . . . a retail job.

Working in a retail environment is, quite obviously, the lowest form of employment. It has no positives at all. It's low paid, it's exhausting, you are dealing with assholes constantly, both with the customers and with your coworkers. It has no redeeming attributes whatsoever. But, to show my parents that I wasn't completely worthless, I decided I needed to get a job and demonstrate my abilities. And, of course, I failed and revealed myself to have no abilities. At least none that were going to help me with my retail career.

It was all utterly doomed from the beginning. For a start, I used my nepotistic tendencies to get the fucking thing. My father had once played golf with Kenneth Cole. So I applied for a role at the Kenneth Cole store in Grand Central Station. On the application I basically wrote, "My dad played golf with your boss," and I got the job. I didn't deserve it and soon proved that I was incapable of executing even the most basic of tasks on any level. But they were too shit scared to fire me. My dad had golfed with Kenneth Cole.

I was seventeen. No one wants to buy shoes from a seventeen-year-old. I was a goofy, panicking, pampered piece of shit who was completely out of his depth. We worked on commission, so this was a toxic, competitive atmosphere. Old, seasoned salesmen who resented anyone taking bread out of their poorly maintained mouths fucking hated me and tried to get me out of the picture immediately.

No one ever showed me how to do anything. Not to fold, not to file, not to ring up a sale, not to find anything in the terrifying basement storeroom that had trains rumbling next to your head and rats fucking merrily on the slingbacks. I had my pride, of course, and refused to show any signs of weakness. So I acted like an utterly arrogant fuck—toward my colleagues; toward my bitch manager, who hated me; toward the customers, who showed no taste at all in selecting this cheap Chinese-manufactured crap to put on their feet. It was a slow-motion car crash taking place every day in my workplace.

After two weeks of trying to fit in, I started to act up. One morning I waltzed in wearing a $700 Hermès belt. It was a thing of beauty and outshone any of the accessories we were desperately trying to sell.

As soon as she spotted it, my bitch manageress took me aside. "You can't wear that here," she told me.

"Why not?"

"It's not an item we stock. What if a customer sees that and wants to buy it?"

"I'd tell them where to find it."

"But we can only promote goods that are designed by Kenneth Cole."

"Really? You see, I don't really think of Kenneth Cole as a designer."

This didn't go down well. Like all management in a franchise like this, she had a near-demonic devotion to the man at the top. He'd probably patted her ass at a Christmas party or a company picnic or something. She probably drooled over his profile in *Fortune* magazine while rubbing one out every night. Who the fuck knows, but she was pissed by my insolence. So I needed to be punished. And she selected the ultimate humiliation for me. I was moved to the ladies' section.

If I was completely unsuited to selling men's shoes, I was almost criminally incapable of selling tasteless shit to fat suburbanites passing through the train station on their way to getting ripped off at a Broadway show while stuffing Milk Duds into their hideous faces. It was farcical.

One glaring problem was that our outlet was pretty small and didn't carry a massive amount of stock. If the customer wanted something in a size or color we didn't carry, we were supposed to call around to other stores and locate what they wanted elsewhere. But, of course, by doing this, we'd lose commission. So I perfected the art of the fake, one-way phone call. I would pretend to telephone our flagship store on Fifth Avenue and see if they had what the customer required. They never did, of course, and most times the dumbfucks would settle for a different color or size and I'd make my money.

Then one day this bitch came in and wanted a handbag. She knew exactly what she wanted, and she instantly hated me. I turned my obsequiousness up to eleven, but she still wasn't happy and acted like I was liberally smeared with dog shit. We didn't have the exact bag she wanted, so I offered to call another store. I picked up the phone and made pretend small talk with the ghost on the other end.

Due to her diligence, I must have laid it on a little too thick and talked for way too long, because the unmistakable sound of a phone that's been off the hook began to blare out. She went ballistic, of course. She accused me of never making the call and attempting to both defraud and humiliate her while I made up some lame excuse about the phone system having a few bugs in it.

She went off and ratted me out to the manageress. Then she stormed out of the store. I knew they were desperate to fire me, so I used every excuse I could think of to save my skin. I claimed she was deranged and had tried to steal the bag and had done the same thing the week before and was an anti-Semite. Any shit that came to mind, basically. I was desperate not to seem like a glorious fuckup in the eyes of my parents and wanted to keep this job for at least the rest of the summer. And so she let me slide. Just. And made it very clear that my next fuckup would be my last.

So it's pretty great that my next fuckup was also my best. I sold a woman two left shoes. Deliberately. Now I'm Al fucking Bundy. Not my finest hour. She came in. She was a bitch. She wanted these particular hideous pumps. I went down to the horror basement to get them. I realized that I'd fucked up and had shown them to another customer previously and not put them away properly. Then I saw an actual rat in the basement stockroom fucking right next to my head and panicked, grabbed two left versions of the same shoe, ran upstairs, and sold them to her. Obviously she came back the next day and was pissed beyond belief. She shouted at me, she shouted at my manager, and she shouted at the imperial logo of Kenneth Cole on the wall.

I knew that was it. I was gone. So I said, "Look, the bitch had two left feet when she was in here yesterday."

And then I walked out.

***

This experience, plus the previously chronicled disaster at New York–Presbyterian Hospital, proved one thing to me: I am not built for conventional work.

It's just not in me. I come from a long line of maverick entrepreneurs. People who never took a train to an office. People who made their own hours and took a day off when they wanted to. People who felt physically sick when someone told them what to do. And I was just like them. It was in my DNA.

Idiots look at my life and assume I'm lazy. I work incredibly hard. But I work hard to make my life easy. I work hard at scoring the best deals on first-class flights. I sweat over getting my face in gossip rags and my name in newspaper columns. I spend considerable time taking the perfect shot to slap up on Instagram. Living my life the way I live it takes work. I just don't have a boss. And I never wear a tie.

I fucking hate ties. Back at Brewster Academy, ties were compulsory. I always wanted to look my best but found it impossible when I had to wear the same tie for ten hours straight every day. They got dirty. They got creased. They looked like shit.

After I finished school, ties represented the norm to me. Only the repressed wear ties. No one wears them out of choice. It's just symbolic of your subservience. Bosses don't bother with ties. Not the big bosses. Their underlings do. It's a marker that denotes "us" and "them." The proles and the privileged. They are disgusting fashion items. People hang themselves with their ties. And I don't blame them.

I had a smoking-hot date. I forget her name. But this bitch was dragging me to a black-tie event. Evening dress compulsory. Tuxedo. My worst fucking nightmare. I hate weddings, I hate formals, and I hate black tie. The problem with tuxedos is that that everyone looks good in them. Some fat fuck fifty-five-year-old or some eighteen-year-old runway model. It's the great leveler. I don't do levelers.

I wanted to stand out from this crowd of penguins. But how the hell do you do that with a tuxedo? I hit up the three Bs: Barneys, Bergdorf, and Bloomingdale's. I wanted to see what they had to offer. Then I found the pocket squares and realized I'd stumbled across something. Pocket squares were perfect. They displayed color and individuality but were formal and refined. I felt like I'd come home.

But the pocket squares I came across were pretty awful. Crappy polyester pieces that I could pick up at Macy's for next to nothing. Or luxury 100 percent silk Hermès objects that retailed for $130. And nothing in between. That's when I realized, like so many times before, that I could slip in between.

This was the perfect product for me. JRL personified. Garish, obnoxious, and the perfect conversation starter. It was eye-catching and different. And a great identifier of assholes. If people knew what a pocket square was, they were worth knowing. If they called it a "handkerchief" or "that colorful thing," you knew they were a fucking schmuck and you should get away from them as quickly as possible. I knew I wanted to get into the pocket-square business, but I just couldn't come up with a name.

Then one night I was lying next to the first rabbi's daughter, mentally masturbating, when I had a eureka moment. Pretentious. I scared the shit out of her by screaming the word. "*Pretentious!*" That would be the perfect fucking name. Truth in advertising. Alliteration to boot. Beat all the haters to the punch. It could never be accused of being pretentious, because it says it right there on the fucking label.

I didn't know a thing about the fashion industry or the fabric trade apart from my few weeks working for Kenneth Cole when I was 17. All I knew was that Kenneth Cole was not the way to do it. I didn't want shitty knockoffs, barely put together in China and accepted with a shrug by idiot customers before they fell apart a couple of months later. I wanted a product that would make people talk.

I took my Hermès pocket square around the globe trying to find the perfect silk. I didn't have a clue, but I got educated by failing. Unfortunately, the countries that make silk are also the countries with the highest proportion of garmentors trying to rip you off. It's a point of pride in India and China to screw poor Jews like myself. But slowly I gained some knowledge and discovered the difference between chiffon and charmeuse. I got wise to bullshit and knew when I wasn't getting the best goods. I'd rub my Hermès through my fingers and then try the material that was being offered to me. I'd learn the weight. If it wasn't as soft, it didn't make the cut.

I finally found my guy in South Korea, just outside Seoul. Outstanding silk that was actually better than what Hermès used. I'd often offer a Pretentious Pocket square alongside a Hermès square in a blind taste test and ask the potential client which pussy they would rather stick their dick in. They've never said Hermès. They'd always want my pussy.

Now I had the perfect material for my product. I just needed one last touch: a label telling its owner they were wearing 100 percent "Fuck You" silk. This colorful language has kept me out of most big-box establishments. But it's important. It's an homage to the most inspirational figure in my fashion life: Ralph Lauren.

The legend goes that Ralph was an up-and-coming tie designer who wanted to make it big. He took his designs into Bloomingdale's, who loved them and wanted to manufacture them in bulk, with one condition: that Ralph take his initials off the tie. He thought for a second, told them to go fuck themselves, and walked straight out of there. That beautiful parable has been an inspiration throughout my mock career. If Ralph hadn't stuck to his guns and offered a great fat FU to the big boys, there'd be no Polo or any of that shit. Can you imagine a Waspy world without Lauren? Horrible thought.

So now my pocket squares are dropped into Grammy gift bags, worn by celebrities, and shipped to twenty-five countries all over the planet, exhibiting the "Fuck You" silk label for all to see. It's sensational. And the perfect advertisement for me. I've never spent a dime on conventional promotion. It's all just me and my smug face, shoving this thing down people's throats. Any opportunity I get, I promote Pretentious Pocket, and that, in turn, promotes me. It's the ideal, never-ending cycle of infamy.

And it makes for a pretentiously perfect present. Once I'd had my first batch of pocket squares, I went on a wild rampage around Manhattan, handing them out to every doorman who had ever crossed me. Those who hated me now liked me. Those who liked me now loved me. It's the perfect thing to give to maître d's and people in positions of respect and authority. It looks amazing and garners compliments every day. And when someone says to them, "Holy shit, what is that thing; it looks incredible," they'll think of me and my punim.

And, as I always espouse, it's the perfect example of working smart, not working hard. The orders and admin are pretty much completely automated. The whole operation takes care of itself. It's passive income. I just have to work on the organic advertising. Which tends to involve me showing off in some way. Which I obviously don't have a problem with. It's a pretty sensational business model. My MBA professors would be proud.

This whole fashion line has also helped to define me. Famous for being famous will only take you so far. Eventually you have to come up with something better than that, or else people will yawn and move on. Say the words "fashion designer" to me, and visions of the biggest douche bag in the world pop into my head. But I guess that's what I do now. I mean, I *do* design the things and pick the names and select the colors. It's all me. So if I'm trapped in a dire conversation with someone I couldn't care less about, telling them I'm a fashion designer gets them off my back. As you know, I hate people asking me what I do. This is an easy out.

Most of all, it's a prop. And I do my best work with props. It's all about being the best. That's why I could never have a day job. I'd never be the best in whatever day job I was crammed into. The best ladies' shoe salesman in the world? Who cares. The best financial administrator or whatever the fuck it was I did at the hospital for two days? Fuck no. I'd be hanging from my tie before the first week was through.

A quick tale. My hatred of ties nearly got me lynched once. I was traveling abroad and in a crowded store sourcing some silk when I was asked if the fabric was for ties.

"Ties? Ties!" I screeched. "I fucking hate ties!"

Of course I'd forgotten I was in Bangkok and soon had a streetful of Thais wanting to kick my ass. That's why I stick to pocket squares.

The Shatner Shimmy

Now, I'm not sure if this story is an example of working conditions, social malfeasance, or the power of celebrity. But before
we begin, let me just clarify that I was just a bystander in this
escapade. The genius behind this grift was not mine. I was
merely an accomplice. But then, as you will realize, I would
say that.

No, this whole swindle involved a close compatriot of mine
who will remain nameless. He's as much of a social criminal as
I am though he occasionally drifts across the line and drops the
"social" part from the title.

I'm going to try and simplify this whole process, as it all got
pretty complicated and involved while still being beautifully
corrupt. The gentleman behind the entire shebang is a professional middleman. He sets up deals, mainly between Israelis
and the Brooklyn-based Hasidic Jews who hate Israelis. Both
sides think they are fucking him, but he's fucking both of them
in an exceptional fashion.

As with most of these stories, a friend of a friend is
involved. In this case a friend of a friend told my fixer colleague
about an Indian-based engineering firm that was seeking some
kind of celebrity for their annual general meeting, which was
taking place in Toronto, home to their North American cor-
porate headquarters. They were willing to spend big to get the
right guy. He asked to be put in touch, as he had the perfect
candidate.

He told the company in India that he could supply William Shatner to their shindig. He'd give a speech, press some
flesh, pose for selfies, the whole fucking rigmarole. Believe it
or not, Captain Kirk is a huge global superstar. He's bigger in
India than not fucking with cows. The bigwigs in Asia got *very*
excited by the thought of Captain Kirk and TJ Hooker making

a personal appearance. They were told that he'd talk to Bill, check his schedule, work out a fee, and get back to them.

Of course, my friend had absolutely no connection with William Shatner at all. All he was to him (and to me) was the guy with a bad rug from the Priceline commercials. But this didn't deter him. He got in touch with Bill's people, claiming to be working for the Indian firm in a PR capacity, and asked how much a personal appearance would set him back. He was told, fairly unbelievably, that the bargain basement rate was $100,000. One hundred thousand dollars for what would equate to three hours' work. Fucking outrageous, but just goes to show the power of celebrity. Shatner is worth over half a *billion* and is eighty-five years old, but he's still willing to shill for this type of shit.

So to recap, my friend was telling the Indians he worked for Shatner and told Shatner that he worked for the Indians. He Jewed Bill down to $75,000 while telling the other side that Shatner wouldn't get out of bed for less than $125,000. He set the whole thing up with a series of heart-pounding conference calls, in which he somehow convinced both sides at once that he was working for the other.

Fuck knows how he pulled it off, but a few days later he called me and asked, "Hey, how would you like to be in William Shatner's entourage?"

Usually I'd never take the backseat in schemes such as this. But when he broke the whole thing down to me, I just had to see what happened. We arrived at the Ritz-Carlton in Toronto, where this brilliant fucker had booked some ludicrous employee rate. So he got a pretty nice setup for seventy-five bucks a night or something. At the Ritz-Carlton. And we were sharing. So everyone there thought we were gay. Small price to pay for such a sweet room.

Then we started working the hotel. My one role in this venture was to case the property and identify any weak spots in the management chain—my particular area of expertise. But there were no weak spots. The general manager was a total pro. Bald, shit-eating grin, eyes everywhere. A bread roll didn't fall on the floor in the dining room without him knowing about it. And he knew we were up to something. He could just smell it.

All we could do was play the Shatner card as much as possible. Here we were, two guys in our twenties claiming to be Bill's agents and protectors. It didn't add up. But we assured them that Mr. Shatner would be arriving in a couple of days and would expect everything to be perfect. We gave them a laughable list of demands: chilled M&M's, no diet sodas in the minibar, that kind of thing. Plus we requested a perpetual tour of the Club Lounge to make sure it met Bill's standards.

The Club Lounge at the Ritz-Carlton is a private area for the elite who want to be kept separated from the general guests. You get free drinks and hors d'oeuvres, and we made it our personal tree house. For three days we filled ourselves for every meal and drained the bar dry. When they tried to close the joint, we'd insist that it wasn't "fully inspected" enough for Shatner's purposes. We were really pushing it. Or my friend was. Except he did not understand the meaning of "pushing." I'm always willing to bend the rules. He just pisses all over them.

Meanwhile, as far as the Indians were concerned, they just needed to be appeased and convinced that Shatner would actually show. And there was no guarantee of this. Anything could go wrong at this point. A quick Google or a couple of awkward questions and this whole fucking thing would crumble like matzo. It was a tightrope we were walking. A tightrope that was on fire. But that's why it was so much fun.

It was the day of Shatner's arrival. The hotel and the general manager were still unconvinced. But we acted like complete pricks anyway. We drilled them on what to do when Mr. Shatner arrived. We had the lobby set up in a certain way. We told the staff not to approach or talk to Mr. Shatner when he appeared (because, of course, he had never met us and had no idea who we were). We even straightened the bellman's tie and told him to be on his best behavior. Just awful stuff.

Meanwhile, at the airport, my compadre was too cheap to cough up the extra seventy bucks to have the limo driver stand by the gate with a sign. So, soon a befuddled, elderly Canadian celebrity was waddling through the Toronto arrivals hall, looking for his ride while being besieged by Trekkies screaming "Live long and prosper!" into his fat, baffled face. Shatner is like a god in Canada.

Eventually Bill found his car and reached the Ritz-Carlton. We were anxiously waiting in the lobby, scoping out the place. The second he stepped out of the car, we darted over to him. All he had to say was something like "What are your names again?" or "Who the fuck are you?" and the staff would have realized we weren't part of his agency, and the whole fucking thing would be over. But luckily, Shatner breathlessly said, "Why didn't you guys meet me at the airport?" which sounded convincing.

As soon as Shatner arrived, everyone's attitude toward us changed. We were totally legitimized, and even the fucking GM, who hadn't bought our bullshit, started kissing our asses.

They had given Bill a really beautiful suite. We'd been given the keys earlier, so he wouldn't have to deal with any of that checking-in bullshit. But my fucking friend, a true grifter, traded our rooms, so Bill and his wife were in our hundred-dollar love nest while we had his fancy suite, which featured a huge gift basket full of upmarket spa products that I purloined and gave to the girl I was banging back in New York.

So stage one was complete. Shatner was in the building and believed we were his handlers, courtesy of the Indian engineering firm. He took a liking to me and asked that I personally escort him around the event (there wasn't much of a security detail). He also took a liking to my pocket square.

"How many of those do you have for me?" he asked. What a *chazer*! He's worth half a billion, and he's still out for every free item he can get his porky mitts on. I gave him a few Pretentious Pocket squares I had on me, which he still wears. If you see a picture of William Shatner at some formal event, he's probably got one of my pocket squares making him look good.

Now we had to get him to the event and make him do his shtick while convincing both parties that we represented the other. I just kept repeating to myself that this wasn't my scheme and the worst that could happen would be my plausible deniability, if that was even a thing. Luckily, when we arrived, practically everyone at this huge annual meeting was getting drunk. They started early and drank hard. And they were manically excited by Shatner's presence.

Unfortunately, Bill was a bust. He spoke in an unenthusiastic fashion for about thirty minutes, took a tour around a few tables, had a few pictures taken, and then wanted to escape as quickly as possible. I tried to keep him there for as long as I could. People had flown in from Delhi to meet Kirk and were happy to slip me hundred-dollar bills to make sure it happened. I made $800 by telling Shatner he *had* to have his picture taken with this guy, who was the head of development or some other important-sounding bullshit title.

But eventually I was worried that the old guy was going to have a stroke or something. His face started to go a peculiar color, and he implored me, "Justin, get me out of here." I was in charge of Shatner's escape, which was as intricate as a POTUS departure from the White House. We got him out of there, through a gaggle of disappointed Indian devotees and into his limo. The bigwigs at the firm were pretty disappointed, but we just had to tell them, "What can we do? It's Shatner—he's crazy." They seemed satisfied by this explanation.

And that should have been it. Shatner flew back out to Los Angeles the next morning, we got out of there with as many Ritz-Carlton products as we could carry, and apparently all the checks cleared. But it wasn't enough for my ballsy friend. Like I said, this fucker doesn't know the meaning of "pushing his luck." He'd gotten all the money from all the parties concerned and made a healthy profit, considering he did barely anything. But a couple of months after the event, he called Shatner's people to complain about their client's performance.

He told them that Bill only spoke for thirty minutes, didn't press enough flesh, was generally disappointing, and in material breach of their contract. He wanted some of the money they'd paid returned to him. Unbe-fucking-lievable. The balls on this guy. At first they refused, and it got ugly. Eventually they relented and returned ten or fifteen grand to him, assuming it would be passed on to the Indian firm. Some hope.

But even this wasn't enough. Then he called the hotel and complained about the shitty room that *we* had given Shatner. Bill was upset by the service and the attention he got and so on. Frankly he was pissed by the whole endeavor, and, as Bill is the spokesman for a large travel company, things could get difficult if he started talking about his unhappiness at the Ritz-Carlton. Again, after some initial reluctance, they relented and compensated him for the full amount. Just a staggering amount of chutzpah. Golf clap.

But for me it was a true learning experience. This was the first time I'd seen this kind of celebrity activity at such close quarters. Even though he was swindled, remember that Shatner got $75,000, flights, meals, and a room at the Ritz-Carlton for basically an hour's work. And people bent over backward to give him exactly what he wanted. He got his cash and a few free pocket squares. He was happy.

It made me want to work harder to get more famous, or more notable. And by work harder, I mean the Shatner version of working harder. Passive income. Turning up, saying a few halfhearted words, and getting out of there with a big fat check. Getting some other idiot to fund my lifestyle and my dedication to traveling the world in luxury while acting like an ass. Now that's working.

CHAPTER 11

GOING GLOBAL

I knew that something was going on in Sweden. I just didn't realize it was me that was going on in Sweden.

The first inkling that my status in Scandinavia had reached gargantuan levels beyond even my necessary level of adulation was when my plane hit the tarmac at Stockholm's Bromma Airport. I was on a JewJetting tour around Europe, causing a stir and generally fucking things up in my own inimitable way. I've always dreamed of the JRL brand spreading across the continent, but I had no idea the extent to which JRL mania had gripped the land of ABBA and IKEA.

I'd sent ahead my manager, Eran, from New York, and I'd been conspiring with Ronnie, my local fixer in Sweden, and they'd dropped hints that something exciting was taking place and I should get there as quickly as I could. But as I looked through the airplane window, I saw a mass of beautifully blond heads collected on the concourse, and I recognized

Eran amongst them. "Strange," I thought, wondering if he had somehow provoked the ire of these Aryans and a lynch mob was in progress. (Things have headed in that direction before. He's that kind of manager.) It was only when I deplaned and hit arrivals that I realized these people were here for me.

I was like fucking Bono or something. There were flowers; there were banners; there was some low-level screaming. And there were girls. The most beautiful girls I had ever seen in my life. They were all elevens, and there's no such thing as an eleven. Mini Heidi Klums with that unmistakably lustful look in their eyes that indicated, "Please understand that I am going to fuck you, and it's going to be great."

I was surrounded by these Swedish nymphos, with Eran and Ronnie valiantly trying to create some space as my fans tried to grab hold of a piece of me. Pieces of paper were slipped into my pocket. Salacious comments were screamed at me in broken English. I had absolutely no idea what was going on, and I fucking loved it.

I eventually got dragged out of the airport, where I was met with a Ferrari bearing my face emblazoned on the hood. I was stunned. When the last thing you're expecting is a Ferrari with your face on it, coming face to face with a Ferrari with your face on it is pretty hysterical. I know that sounds like utter bullshit, and I can barely believe it myself, so here's a photo as proof . . .

© 2013 Eran Silverberg

And I know you think I've mocked that up with Photoshop, but I swear on my undeserved sense of accomplishment that thing was sitting right there in the airport parking lot waiting for me to enter it. And yes, it did say "I'm Justin Ross Lee. Who the fuck do Jew think you are?" Pretty classy. This was used to whisk me away from my adoring fans and to my fully comped hotel suite. Once there, Ronnie opened up a bilingual folder that set out my next seventy-two hours in Stockholm. Every minute of every day was allocated. There were to be nightclub appearances, photo shoots, interviews, business meetings, and a wide range of other activities. Even my showers had been time-tabled. I was still (and remain) in a complete state of shock.

I wondered if this pace could actually be maintained, or if Ronnie was full of shit with his folder of fun and, in truth, demand for JRL in a country that I'd yet to visit was that high. But you know what? It could and it was. My stock was hot. The next three days were the most insane and demanding of my life. Every single second was dedicated to inflating my ego as much as humanly possible.

As well as the Ferrari, a whole fleet of vehicles appeared, all branded with my gorgeous visage and used to transport me and my entourage from luxurious place to luxurious place. There was even a helicopter with my likeness on the fuselage, which was used to fly me over the archipelago. Why? I don't fucking know. It was all part of the adventure. I talked to media outlets and Sweden's biggest newspapers, trying to explain this new JRL phenomenon to a baffled collection of journalists (even though I was as clueless as they were at this point). I'd visit four or five different nightclubs each evening, have a cocktail thrust into my hand, meet a few excited Swedes, and then be dragged off to the next one.

On one occasion I pulled up outside some swanky spot in my branded Ferrari and emerged from the backseat wearing a robe, like I'd just rolled out of bed and straight to the club. Now I'd evolved into Hefner or something. I disrobed, hurled it at a gaggle of girls waiting outside, and strutted into the place like the hot piece of shit that I guess I was at the moment. I mean, this kind of behavior was jet-fuel dangerous. Even I knew it was going to have a damaging effect on my self-delusion. I didn't even think that was possible.

Meals were accompanied with gift bags. Appearances felt like film premieres. The hotel staff treated me like the A-list celebrity I was oddly perceived to be. Everyone dedicated themselves to my pleasure and comfort. It was magical. And then there were the girls.

Sweden has to have the most attractive women in the world. Hands down. No competition. Blonde bombshells who just exude youth, class, and an unhealthy obsession with the opposite sex. They had absolutely no bullshit attached to them at all. No game playing. No agendas. They just want to fuck anyone famous and non-Swedish.

These girls were happy to approach me and make it painfully clear, in no uncertain terms, that they were available to be taken home so I could do unspeakable things to them as hard as possible. Which I did. For the first two nights, at least. Forty-eight hours into my Swedish adventure, I was starting to burn out. And I never burn out. I'm JRL. But these women had fucked all of the energy out of me. I was a spent husk of a Jew. So I had to do something that I had never done before and never thought I would do ever in my life until the plug got pulled: I had to turn down pussy.

Not just any pussy. We are talking about the finest pussy on the planet. Virtual supermodels at my hotel door at two in the morning insisting that I fuck them. Women that looked like Olympic beach-volleyball competitors crossed with Victoria's Secret models. Perfect specimens of femininity. Young, blond, and full of fun. But, sadly, not full of me. I just had to say no. For the sake of my sanity and my dick, which was completely numb due to all this Scandinavian friction, I had to send them away. It was like some sort of perfect living hell.

So, after three days of this adulation and sexual abuse, I was finally dragged to the airport. As a final example of my lasting and powerful fame in this land, the woman at the check-in desk didn't even ask to look at my passport. "Ah yes," she said, "I recognize you," and she typed for a second and then whisked me to the front of the security line, as if I were an Academy Award winner or Nobel laureate.

My next stop was Amsterdam, supposedly the debauched hotbed of Europe, filled to the brim with weed and clubs and hookers in shop windows. But I didn't even leave my room. I spent the whole trip trying to recover from what Sweden had done to me.

It was my first hands-on experience of celebrity. And I
loved it. Oh, Sweden.

***

Scandinavia seems the ideal location to launch a total global
conquest. They "get" me there in ways lots of other places
don't. I've spent a lot of time mulling over why this socialist
paradise signed up so readily to the JRL experience. Why they
came flocking to see me at the airport. Why they followed me
through the streets like a flock of overtaxed sheep. Why so
many of them just wanted to fuck me. Over there it's a competitive sport. I finally surmised that I was a legitimate A-lister
in Sweden because I was the antithesis of Sweden.

This is a country that taxes you at 70 percent, where the
state subsidizes everything, and where no one is expected to
showcase more than others. The idea that some hideous American would parachute into their country, act like a total douche
bag, and be given so much stuff for free without paying a penny
freezes their blood like a particularly grim Arctic winter. And
that's why the kids love it.

It's like punk rock. To the millennials who worship me in
Sweden, I go against everything that their country stands for.
I'm the perfect anti–role model. Rich, privileged, and, worst
of all, American. So, as the epitome of everything that's wrong
with my homeland, I'm treated like a god. In a country that
doesn't have much of a celebrity culture beyond the odd tennis
star or singing group, I embodied the most baffling variety of
celebrity. Someone without a product to promote or foist on
you except for myself. In a nation like Sweden, that is unfathomable. And attractive.

They adore celebrities over there, as so few stray that far
north. And even when they do, they merely wave on the way

to the airport after promoting their latest piece of shit on local TV for ten minutes. I was a celebrity who was almost accessible. They could get within a few feet of me and see me in the flesh. They could bask in my glory and dream of being JRL. Which, after all, is what everyone wants. I was the bizarro version of a typical Swede—Jewish, opinionated, and decadent. Highly aspirational.

So Sweden played into my palms like a drunk shiksa at a Vegas nightclub. And after getting a taste of this notoriety level, I wanted more. But I'm not crazy. I've been doing this shit too long. There's one thing that's vitally important to remember: you can't please everyone all of the time, as I believe Snooki once said through a mouthful of cocks. And I'm not talking about the finely balanced 49/51 split of people who either love or despise me. I'm talking about people who just don't get it at all. There is an unacceptable number of them around the planet. And if I readily identify a nation as not being worthy of the full JRL experience, then I won't waste my energies on its citizens. At least not yet. But that doesn't mean that they can't still be used and abused.

In most English-speaking nations, I am beloved and revered for my sensational sense of humor, devastating wordplay, and trenchant wit. That obviously goes without saying. And whether you find my shtick funny or not (and if you don't, then perhaps you can find another use for that stick up your ass), you at least recognize that others do.

But there are areas of the world (and I appreciate that most in the flyover states may find this hard to believe) where English is not readily spoken. In these so-called foreign nations, my razor-sharp shtick can sometimes get lost in translation. My material never works quite so well when it's transformed into French or Swahili. But that doesn't mean those places aren't eligible for my particular JRL brand of charm. I just have to find other ways in which to exploit them.

If it's a particularly scenic location, then it can be used as a basis for some aspirational tourism. Sure, they might not have any idea of who I am in Malaysia, but if I post a picture of myself on Instagram sitting next to an infinity pool with some garish cocktail in my hand and the rainforest off in the distance, it helps to maintain the myth of JRL. How the fuck did he manage to get to that place? How can I get there, too? How can I be just like JRL? I've often wondered the same . . .

It doesn't matter that they have no idea who I am in these places. In fact, it's really helpful they don't. As the international renown of JRL increases, it's harder and harder to pull off the social crimes that I've patented and used with such success. All these countries have to do is look pretty in the pictures and let me get away with my legendary douchery. I'll take care of the rest.

Then there are other places where they get me and know me—they just don't appreciate me. Like in France. Not everyone loves Americans in France and, unlike the far more sensible Swedes, don't want to love Americans. And so they view me as some sort of "ultimate American" and as such pretty much the worst human being alive. Canal Plus, a TV channel over there, ran a feature on me during some prime-time magazine show, concerning my skyrocketing fame and unsolicited worldwide omnipresence. It seemed more of a cautionary tale than the raw propaganda that I favor. But I didn't really give a fuck, as it helped to sell a few pocket squares.

That's the beautiful thing about the Pretentious Pocket: it's such a versatile luxury item. As well as being the perfect gift for irate doormen, club owners, and restaurateurs, it also looks good absolutely everywhere. All over the globe, people wear suits and want to add a dash of vibrancy to their dress. And each time I get some press in a far-flung land, my sales in that location suddenly boom. Even if it's an article decrying me as Jewish Satan.

So that's another way I can exploit nations that refuse to adopt the JRL ethos as their new way of life. They may hate me and fail to understand me, but oddly they still buy my pocket squares. And the bank of JRL is happy to take any form of currency from anywhere. Liking me is not a stipulation when handing over your cash. I've shipped everywhere from Venezuela to Cameroon. Maybe they spotted me on *Millionaire Matchmaker*, which I turned into a forty-four-minute-long Pretentious Pocket infomercial, or in some local tabloid rag that picked up one of my celebrity-baiting stories and smeared my face all over their pages. That happened to me in Croatia. I still don't know how or why. But they ordered some pocket squares, so I couldn't give a fuck.

And I do want to go further. Because I love to travel. Jew-Jetting may be all about the flight and the experience, but I have a passion for exploring new places that haven't troubled me before. I want to invade and colonize these unknown quantities. Like China, for instance. I'd love to flood China with my products and my philosophy. Imagine. A few billion JRL clones throwing off the shackles of Mao and adopting the philosophy of Me. There's a lot of people and yuan floating around that ludicrously massive landmass. I've just got to get my hands on it.

The Swedish adventure proved to me that it could be done. This insane journey I've been on and my attempts at self-generated fame on my terms and using my methods can obviously have the desired effect. It turned me into an A-list figure in the flesh. In the United States, I'm followed, loved, despised, and envied. I'm stopped several times walking through an airport to have a selfie taken. I enjoy all the perks of fame and use it to maintain a healthy lifestyle. But in Sweden I tasted true celebrity. Brad and Angelina levels of madness and decadence. It was exhausting, but I lapped it up.

Welcome to Charm School

Look, I'm an asshole. That has been unequivocally expressed and proven time and time again over these pages. I look like a douche bag, I act like a douche bag, and I live like a douche bag. And if I wasn't already aware of it, there are plenty of people out there willing to let me know on a continual basis.

But unlike many of the douche bags that pollute this planet, I'm self-aware. Being a screaming asshole for twenty-four hours a day toward every single human being you encounter might sound like a lot of fun, but the returns are going to be diminishing.

Total fucking dickwads soon develop a reputation, and, unsurprisingly, people avoid them. Unless you are so rich or so powerful that you can treat every single person you meet like utter shit without any form of consequence, then you need to limit your assholery to those who truly deserve it.

This applies across the planet. No matter where you are, you don't take it out on a busboy at the bottom of the chain, as they are the people whom you rely on. Or, alternatively, they are the ones who can really help when you want to extricate yourself from some bullshit situation or plan to undertake some convoluted social scam. You always need friends or accomplices.

As everybody knows, the valets hold all the power in Vegas. They know where the bodies are buried, they know who is sleeping with whom, and they know the best places to get things done. And this applies across the board. If you're trying to get some vital information or some shit for free, you're not going to approach the CEO of Starwood or United Airlines. You go to the guy behind the bar or pushing a broom or working security. And you charm the shit out of him.

I've managed to get so much free crap and unparalleled access by being decent to someone who gets treated like shit for eight straight hours a day. You just have to be understanding and offer them the tiniest glimmer of respect. Because that never happens. All the time people who look exactly like me walk up to them and treat them like gum squashed on the bottom of their Louboutins. You offer them a sympathetic shoulder to cry on, and they'll love you like a lonely fat chick at a wedding.

The security guard at my prep school, the taxi driver in Hartford who would personally chauffeur me everywhere, bouncers at Manhattan nightclubs, the guys who clear the tables at the sushi restaurant I use like an office, and thousands and thousands of others—I've got them all in my pocket, because I don't act like a total ass around them. And I make them laugh.

Look, it's totally possible that you can laugh a woman into bed. And you can certainly laugh a service worker into doing your bidding. You make a joke about their boss, you offer up some zinger about the customers, or you make some crack about their wife. You add a bit of humor to the endless dreariness of their day. And they'll love you for it!

And the beauty of all this is that it's universal. In fact, it's more effective when you're overseas. I don't know if you're aware of this, but Americans have something of a reputation when it comes to foreign travel. Basically everybody fucking hates us, or they're oddly fascinated by us. This is because compared to our cosmopolitan European neighbors, hardly any Americans travel abroad, and the ones that do represent us poorly, as they're so far out of their comfort zones and there's not a fucking Olive Garden on every corner. Rather than try to speak to people rationally, they just bark at them in hopes that the increased volume will suddenly make them understand English.

So if you act like a genuine human being to our foreign cousins, they'll be both amazed and eternally grateful. And it does something for our standing abroad. No longer do we have to pretend to be Canadians or mute. Perhaps if we don't all act like enormous pricks the second our passports get stamped, not only would it oil the wheels of travel, but Americans wouldn't be number one on the shit list in every country on the planet, too.

Of course, I'm not Mother Teresa. Sometimes people just deserve to get treated like shit. And sometimes acting like an utter fucking jerk can be equally effective in getting your own way (go back and check out the full-circle approach for pointers). And sometimes people are just dicks and need to be talked to like dicks. If the situation demands, I can be the most aggressive, annoying, weaselly cunt in this hemisphere. Honestly, I don't give a shit. If someone needs to be yelled at, I'll scream my fucking lungs inside out. But that shit's exhausting. I don't *start* from that position. But I can click into that mode pretty fucking quickly when provoked.

So you charm from the bottom up. Start with the little people, and then move on to the middle management. Have some wisecracks ready. Empathize with the misery of their situation. Make sure they understand that you understand. They are not just some walking, mop-holding pieces of meat that can be barreled over or ignored. There'll be plenty of opportunities to act like an asshole, don't you worry. And if you don't get what you want, you turn on the wrath.

CHAPTER 12

IN CONCLUSION, YOU'RE WELCOME

I felt the most suitable way to conclude this life-changing and vital document that I assume you'll keep close to your person at all times and consult at moments of spiritual crisis was to speak to someone who has shaped, influenced, and inspired me. A human being who has completely altered my worldview and helped me develop into the near-perfect Jew (you see, I do have some humility) you see before you. But after an extensive search I realized no one was appropriate. Except me. And so I sat myself down and probed my consciousness deeply for the purposes of this book and the betterment of man. You're welcome.

Who are you?

I am Justin Ross Lee, a.k.a. JRL, a.k.a. seat 1A, a.k.a. the forefather of the field of JewJetting, a.k.a. the ego that attacked New York.

And what do you do?

Come on, Justin, you know I hate that question. You already know the answer: simply as I please.

I'm sorry, I'm going to have to press you.

You wouldn't be the first. Practically every shiksa in the tristate area has tried. OK, fine, *Wikipedia* states "haberdasher." But, in fact, I'm an explorer. I travel the world and make an impression on people. A big fucking impression.

Some might question your definition of an explorer.

Hey, look, I drop myself into completely uncharted territories and bullshit my way through unnavigated waters for the greater good, using only my innate charm and unparalleled wardrobe. I conquer places people have never even heard of and vanquish areas people fear to tread. I'm like Columbus with better diplomacy, and fewer kills. That sounds like a fucking explorer to me.

Very impressive. And please accept my apologies. But how can you possibly accomplish all these amazing things?

Great question. In order to travel the planet in the way that I am accustomed and use the world as my own personal plaything,

I have developed a series of systems—as this book has hopefully taught you—to thoroughly infiltrate institutions required
to help me succeed. In that way I am a pioneer. And, some have
said, a virtuoso.

**I can completely understand that, but where would you like
all this enterprise and brilliance to lead?**

Well, Justin, I simply can't understand why airlines and the
greater travel industry aren't constantly trying to climb into
bed with me to help them let me create a better way. I've got all
the answers. They'd have to recognize their deficits and admit
defeat. The industry is sick. And I'm the cure. I'm Frank Abagnale with an MBA.

So would you consider him a role model?

Nah. Role models are bullshit. The only role model anyone
should have is me.

And are you a role model to anyone?

There are myriad tiny little JRLs out there watching me doing
my thing on Facebook, picking up my tips. I get messages from
people saying they've quit their jobs and started to follow my
teachings like I'm the Dalai Lama or something. It's scary. I'm
shaping minds. I'm influencing the next generation. I'm setting
trends. That actually frightens the shit out of me!

**So the thought of a legion of proto-JRLs JewJetting and
dry-humping their way around the world concerns you?**

As long as I am safely on a yacht somewhere, watching all this shit go down from afar, anyone can do whatever they want. That's always been my philosophy.

Let's get a little deeper . . .

I say that a lot.

Can you remember a particular moment that inspired your remarkable life?

Yeah. I was thirteen or so. I'd just been thrown off this rich-Jewish-kid teen tour for biting some postpubescent girl's nipple. They kicked me out in the middle of nowhere. Somewhere beige. Colorado, I think. I remember people wearing a lot of big hats, which thoroughly disturbed me. My parents, not for the last time, had to swoop in and come to the rescue. They had to pay to fly me home. Coach. I wasn't impressed.

I had nothing to lose, so I went up to the United Airlines gate jockey and spun them some completely bullshit story of hardship and misery and a rare genetic leg condition that required me to have an upgrade. And it completely fucking worked. The moment he tore up my original ticket and handed me a fresh one marked "1A" was the moment I realized that you can always take whatever you decide to take. I scored my first upgrade at thirteen, and I'll never forget it. You don't need to accept what is offered to you like a putz. There's always something better if you fight for it. I was barely a bar mitzvah, and I'd learned an incredibly important lesson.

So that set you on this path?

Partly. It was my first time rearranging the system. Grabbing victory from the jaws of defeat. So rather than skulk home with my newly descended testes between my legs, I traveled back in style. It felt fucking huge.

You spun gold out of shit?

Very well put. You're a bright guy. Yes, this set me on the path of never having setbacks. No matter what happens, you can always spin it into success. Look at me and Star Jones. She got me kicked out of a polo event. I looked like a schmuck. I felt like shit; it was hugely embarrassing. But I turned that incident into coverage. It was a valuable lesson. A kick in the balls can always be turned into a wonderfully erotic experience.

What does your family make of all this?

I think they used to be concerned, then they were just confused, but now they "get it." Trying to explain the role of JRL to the woman who changed your diapers was a tough sell. But you can't worry about what other people think. Regardless, my mom and dad truly are the greatest.

Did your childhood scar you?

Literally. When I was in fourth grade, I tried to impress this girl I had a crush on by attempting a complicated Rollerblading maneuver in front of her and a group of kids. I fell on my face and chipped a tooth. And I got laughed at by jocks. But this was another educational experience. You never impress anyone by doing the same shit as everyone else. You need to be unique. I'm always going to suck at Rollerblading, but I will always succeed at being different.

So Rollerblading isn't your secret skill?

No, my secret skill is winning people over and getting them to do my bidding even though I come across as an obnoxious, pretentious prick. I should be someone that you immediately want to fuck over and hate—but select people love me! How do I manage that? Well, it's a skill.

Is there anyone it's not worth winning over?

Kids. Fucking kids. Especially on airplanes. What's the point? They're annoying and bring very little to the conversation.

Is there any individual that you couldn't win over?

That dipshit Dean Doucheborn. From my prep school. I just couldn't break that Christ fucker. But I could make his life a misery, so I decided to use that method instead. On a completely unrelated note, I find the idea of a grown man who decides to spend his entire life surrounded by adolescents incredibly creepy. Just saying.

So your school days weren't the best days of your life?

Anyone who thinks that way must have had a particularly disappointing adulthood.

Obviously it's hard to beat being you, but would you consider ever being anyone else for a day?

Howard Stern. He was social media before there was social media. He was loved, hated, and at the same time he was relevant. He grew into success having a soapbox tall enough that he can't be avoided. If not Stern, then maybe Bill Clinton. Who wouldn't want to have lunch with Bill Clinton? The shit that guy must have seen and dealt with. It would be fun to bounce ideas around with that legend.

Would you ever be tempted into politics?

Congressman Lee? Can you fucking imagine? No, I've done too much shit. My skeletons aren't even in the closet—they're all available online. No thanks. Politicians make rules for everyone else. I make up my own and then strive to break them. I don't think anyone would vote for that.

What if you could be a woman for a few hours? What would be the first thing you'd do?

Thoroughly disrespect myself. Assuming I was a hot chick, I'd get whatever was coming to me. People are just instantly nice to you if you're a hot chick. Good genetics are like winning the lottery. Everything is provided. There's an entire industry in Los Angeles based around just being a hot chick. You don't need to possess any discernible talent. Just look good. Holy shit, could you imagine? If my brains were in the body of a shiksa with an incredible rack? I'd take over the fucking world! The only problem with being a hot chick, though, is all the responsibility. You have to keep looking immaculate, or it will all crumble away. I'm not sure I could face doing that. I mean, let's not kid ourselves. I have to have a pretty hardcore regimen just to keep JRL looking like JRL—but it's nothing compared to a woman's.

So you're not a fan of responsibility?

The more responsibility I can shed, the happier I am. That's my idea of a perfect day. Waking up and realizing that I have absolutely no obligation to anyone or anything unimportant to me. Just doing exactly what I want to do. Most people, if they suddenly decided to do that, their whole house of cards would start to tumble. Their entire existence is based around a shitload of but/ifs. I live right on the edge of those but/ifs, and the more of them I can eradicate from my life, the better it is. No responsibility, no repercussions. No clocking in. That's freedom.

But freedom to do what?

Travel! Live. Experience the world, not your hometown. That's what it's all about! To get out of this or any time zone and into another, often.

Is there anywhere you haven't been to that you'd like to visit?

More of Africa. That place needs to be JRL'd. Unlimited potential. Yeah, if I could get my hands on big chunks of Africa, that would be sweet. But, y'know, not in a *12 Years a Slave* way.

Is there anywhere you never want to visit?

America. Been there, done that. As soon as I hear someone who sounds like me, I just want to run in the opposite direction. I'm aware of the flyover states. I've seen pictures. Walmart. That's all you need to know. I travel to broaden my horizons.

What do you say to people who are frightened to travel?

It's all over for you. Go back to your myopic nonexistence.

But you must have been to some dangerous places. Aren't you ever afraid?

Oh, sure. I've been to places that trade in body parts. I was held at knifepoint for hours in Cambodia. I've been targeted in every hemisphere. But that's all part of the fun. Keeps you on your toes.

If you were a victim of crime, what would you be most afraid of losing?

My matzo balls. Without them, I'm nothing. Truly, I could manage without anything else. And as I mentioned, I've been to places where they trade in even larger organs. Everything I do, everything I achieve, stems from balls. They are the source of all my power. You need balls to do my job.

What's the best advice you've been given?

Don't listen to advice.

And who said it to you?

Me. If I'd followed advice, I wouldn't be doing what I'm doing. I guess that's more of a question. All you can do is do what you want. Whatever makes you happy. And then find a way to keep doing it. If you live for boning women, find a way to monetize it. Male gigolo may just be the career for you. Then write a book about it.

If you're doing the opposite of what people expect you to do, then you're probably on the right track. Obviously, if people are telling you to stop strangling hookers, that's not JRL telling you to strangle a boatload of hookers. But again, if it makes you happy, who am I to judge?

JRL, you have had many fantastic accomplishments in your life, but what would you consider your greatest?

Subversion. Convincing people, rightfully, that they shouldn't do the thing that they are expected to do. Molding the minds of the young to embrace counterconvention. Nothing makes me prouder than fan mail from someone who says, "I want to be just like you." It's an awesome responsibility. And as you know, I don't care for responsibility. But someone has to lead these kids to the promised land.

Is that how you want to be remembered? As a molder of young minds?

"Remembered" makes it sound like I'm going somewhere. And I'm not going anywhere—I'm going everywhere.

How do you want the third act of the JRL story to play out?

Watching people worldwide doing what I've taught them to do. Being synonymous with beating the system. Whenever there's a story about shtupping the great institutions of the world, I want to be the first one that CNN calls for comment. I want to be the godfather of consultancy. And I never want to stagnate. I'm going to be always moving. Like a shark. Traveling every-where with my best girl beside me.

Best girl? Really? Is this a new side to JRL?

Listen, I've ODed on sexcapades. The young me would never believe that could even be possible. But I hit the pussy pinnacle. There's only so much you can do and have done to you. And don't get me wrong, I loved every minute. But there's nothing better than having a shiksa beside you that you can trust. Someone you can show the world to. Traveling alone is great, but there's a certain intimacy to seeing a place through someone else's eyes. Someone who makes you a better you. That's true love.

And how do you see JRL's grand finale taking place?

Ironically. I assume I'll be on a plane. Why not go out doing what you enjoy? I just don't ever want to die waiting in line. Can you imagine how depressing that would be?

And what would you like written on your tombstone?

"I can see up your skirt . . ."

JRL, it's been an absolute pleasure.

Thank you, Justin. I completely agree.

ACKNOWLEDGMENTS

"Normal" people do what is expected of them. They embrace convention. They accept what seat or room they're assigned. They don't get excited by unattended housekeeping carts or holes in loyalty programs, and they never seem to challenge the status quo. I dedicate this book to anyone who has ever been told to act "normal." If you've spent your life working harder at being yourself as opposed to the easier task of changing to be someone else, fuck normal. This book is written for you—and for the following people.

My beautiful and loving girlfriend, **Kate**, who has always accepted my world of eccentricities, without waver.

My adoring mother, the most devoted and caring woman on this earth. Thank you for understanding.

My brilliant coauthor, **Dale Shaw**, for his British wit, literary talent, patience, and therapy.

My talented agent, **Lisa Kopel**, for her resilience and dedication to our project from its inception.

Our publisher, **Inkshares,** and their appointments, for creating a judgment-free home for a first-time author who never fit in.

ABOUT THE AUTHOR

Justin Ross Lee is an entrepreneur, travel expert, and social media provocateur who has redefined the notion of modern fame and celebrity. He has created and cultivated a persona both online and off. Flying in excess of 250,000 miles per year, he has come to the attention of mainstream media and has subsequently been featured heavily in the popular press.

Covered by a myriad of magazines and in the pages of the *New York Times* and the *New York Post*, JRL has headlined on such networks as E!, Bravo, VH1, and Fox News. His controversial appearance on *The Millionaire Matchmaker* was the most critically acclaimed episode of the season. He is the founder and purveyor of Pretentious Pocket, a world-renowned pocket-square company with sales in over two dozen countries.

LIST OF PATRONS

Don't You Know Who I Think I Am? was made possible in part by the following grand patrons who preordered the book on Inkshares.com. Your support was indispensable, and I am beyond grateful.

Alberto C. Butcher

Amit Vaswani

Andrew Thompson

Ann Jensen

Benjamin Kass

Brandon Morton

Brandon Slagle

Chad Anderson

Christoph Jung

Cobey L. Parnell

David Haas

Dirk A. Sanders

Dorit Pour

Eric D. Jenkins

Eric K. Ng

Eric Marchwinski

Evan Singh Luthra

Federico H. Cabotage

Garry E. Nelson

Geoffrey Bernstein

Geoffrey Harris

Hunter Lee Naill

Ian D. Scherzer

James Katz

Jan Tore Borgersen

Jason Reid

Jay Jay

Jeff Crays

Jeffrey Catlett
João Gasparian De Almeida
   Mello
Jodi S. Harris
Kyle Pukylo
LC Rep
Mark Anthony
Markus Virta
Michael Hedman
Michael Kisil
Mindy Carter
Noel Bollmann
Pmessina246
Richard A. Schnase

Roberto Cardenas
Ronnie Skold
Ross Jones
Salvador Robles
Sheikku1
Stephen Cugliari
Steve Teitter
Tor Andre Espedal Vorpenes
Vandi Huynh
Vincent Dolliole Jr.
Wayne Quek
WLE Koster
www.bart.la

INKSHARES

Inkshares is a crowdfunded book publisher. We democratize publishing by having readers select the books we publish—we edit, design, print, distribute, and market any book that meets a preorder threshold.

Interested in making a book idea come to life? Visit inkshares.com to find new book projects or start your own.